# Teaching Literature in Modern Foreign Languages

# Teaching Literature in Modern Foreign Languages

**Edited by**
**Fotini Diamantidaki**

BLOOMSBURY ACADEMIC
LONDON · NEW YORK · OXFORD · NEW DELHI · SYDNEY

BLOOMSBURY ACADEMIC
Bloomsbury Publishing Plc
50 Bedford Square, London, WC1B 3DP, UK
1385 Broadway, New York, NY 10018, USA

BLOOMSBURY, BLOOMSBURY ACADEMIC and the Diana logo are trademarks of
Bloomsbury Publishing Plc

First published in Great Britain 2019
Copyright © Fotini Diamantidaki and Contributors, 2019

Fotini Diamantidaki has asserted her right under the Copyright, Designs and Patents
Act, 1988, to be identified as Editor of this work.

Cover image © triocean/ iStock

Bloomsbury Publishing Plc does not have any control over, or responsibility for, any
third-party websites referred to or in this book. All internet addresses given in this book
were correct at the time of going to press. The author and publisher regret any
inconvenience caused if addresses have changed or sites have ceased to exist,
but can accept no responsibility for any such changes.

A catalogue record for this book is available from the British Library.

A catalog record for this book is available from the Library of Congress.

ISBN: HB: 978-1-3500-6301-3
PB: 978-1-3500-6300-6
ePDF: 978-1-3500-6303-7
eBook: 978-1-3500-6302-0

Typeset by Newgen KnowledgeWorks Pvt. Ltd., Chennai, India
Printed and bound in Great Britain

To find out more about our authors and books visit www.bloomsbury.com
and sign up for our newsletters.

# Contents

# Acknowledgements

With thanks to:
Marian Carty: Robert Desnos activities
Alyssa Hickson: Doña pitu piturra exercise
Ciara Mulvenna: Le Petit Nicolas materials
Lisa Panford: La Paloma activities

# Notes on Contributors

**Verna Brandford** is Secondary PGCE Languages Lecturer, Teach First London Modern Foreign Languages Subject Lead, UCL Institute of Education. Following a three-year teacher training course, Verna taught French, German and Spanish in a number of challenging London secondary schools, including three as head of department. She has also taught French to primary school pupils and adults. She has taught in France and Germany. She was a primary/secondary advisory teacher and subsequently worked as a local authority consultant advisor/inspector after training as an Ofsted inspector for languages. She has also led and taught on the Bachelor of Education module Teaching and Learning in Classrooms and was the professional coordinator for the Secondary PGCE course. Her research interests are the development of the Storyline approach in foreign language classrooms as part of a PhD thesis and pupils 'bucking the trend of underachievement' particularly in modern foreign languages.

**Colin Christie** is a lecturer (scholarship) in Modern Languages Initial Teacher Education at the University of Aberdeen. Before that, he was lecturer in Languages in Education and subject leader for the PGCE Languages course at University College London Institute of Education. Prior to this, he worked at the University of Cumbria's London base, mainly on the Modern Languages PGCE. He has held a number of advisory positions, including as a Key Stage 3 consultant in the London Borough of Hackney and has produced teaching resources in a variety of media. He has also worked in schools and colleges in different roles, such as a languages development project coordinator in a language college and a head of department. His PhD thesis was on the topic of spontaneous learner target language talk in the languages classroom and his academic interests include the teaching and learning of modern languages, in particular pupil use of the target language, the development of spontaneous target language talk and the inclusion of meaningful content in modern languages lessons. He has been a member of the ALL ITET Steering Group linking language teaching and teacher education. Recent publications include Christie and Conlon's *Success Stories from Secondary Foreign Languages Classrooms: Models from London School Partnerships with Universities* (2016) and Christie's 'Speaking Spontaneously in the Modern Foreign Languages Classroom: Tools for Supporting Successful Target Language Conversation' (2016).

**Fotini Diamantidaki** is a lecturer in Education at the UCL Institute of Education, University of London, UK. She received a PhD in applied linguistics from Nice Sophia Antipolis University in France, an MA in applied linguistics from the same University, a BA from the Aristotle University in Thessaloniki, Greece, and a Post Graduate Certificate in Education (PGCE) from the

UCL Institute of Education in London, UK. Her research interests include the integration of literature in the language classroom in combination with the use of internet and the digital technologies as well as the integration of world languages into the curriculum. Teacher education pedagogy and learning how to teach are fundamental strands to her research interests. New recent research interests involve the growth of Mandarin teacher education in England, cultural and intercultural awareness and understanding in secondary classroom contexts and in higher education and mentoring in teacher education. Most recent publications concern the teaching of Mandarin Chinese in secondary, *Mandarin Chinese Teacher Education: Issues and Solutions* (2018), and for primary school, 'The teaching and learning of Chinese in primary schools in England: developing a new learning approach to support intercultural understanding' (2017), in Race, and 'Using literature in the KS3 foreign language classroom' (2016) in Christie and Conlon. She currently teaches on the PGCE Languages course at the postgraduate level, and is involved in the supervision of pre-service MA TESOL students and doctoral students. She has taught French in London secondary schools and pedagogy on other teacher education routes over the years. She has successfully co-launched a project on teaching literature in secondary school classrooms in England called 'London Partnership launches literature' and thanks to it, the PGCE Languages team has received a British Academy Award for its innovative and engaging nature.

**Jennifer Eddy** is a tenured assistant professor of world language education at Queens College, City University of New York. For twenty-five years, Eddy has taught undergraduate and graduate courses for teacher certification and has directed seminars for university and high school faculty on curriculum and assessment design. Her research focuses on performance assessment, transfer and intercultural competence in articulated curriculum design.

In 2004, Eddy developed the framework *Uncovering Curriculum: Assessment Design Advancing Performance and Transfer* (UC: ADAPT), integrating backward design/UbD with the national standards. This design uses overarching intercultural perspectives to unfold thematic curriculum with performance assessment for vertical articulation. Schools and universities have implemented this design for language departments and teacher education programs.

Dr Eddy authored *Sonidos, Sabores, Y Palabras* (2006, Heinle/Cengage), the first book using songs as culturally authentic material within a backward design framework. Her work is featured in the NCLRC publication, *Teaching World Languages: A Practical Guide* (2014), JNCOLCTL (2015), and in the NECTFL volume on Intercultural Competence (2017). Eddy composed multimedia curriculum guides for the New York City Department of Education and now is project director for the New York State Department of Education designing professional development materials for world language teachers.

**Steven Fawkes** moved to the north-east to do his teacher training after studying languages at the University of Cambridge, and still lives in Durham where he began teaching languages in 1977. His thirteen years of teaching in a Comprehensive School in Durham City were followed by three years as a curriculum support teacher in the county, supporting curriculum development for languages across mainstream and special provision during the implementation of the first National Curriculum. At the same time, he was founder secretary of the NE branch of ALL (Association for Language Learning) – he continues to volunteer for ALL to this day. Professionally, Steven then moved to London to work as education officer for schools (languages) at the BBC; this work involved the development of TV, radio, print and internet resources for languages in schools as well as evaluation and training work with teachers. Here he was involved in award-winning projects such as Tobu-KS3 Japanese online, GCSE Bitesize and Something Special. Later, Steven also took the lead on resources for special education and finally moved to managing the overview of policy in the whole schools area. Subsequently, he worked in Initial Teacher Education and teacher continuing professional development (CPD). He has twice been president of the association, and he is now a trustee and membership officer; in 2013, he was elected as a fellow of the association. He is chair of the ALL branch in the north-east of England and is closely involved with the work of several special interest groups within the association (including currently the Initial Teacher Education SIG and the Primary Steering Group). Steven writes regularly for *Languages Today* magazine and ALL online publications; he has written also extensively in the past for CiLT, BBC and TES as well as authoring books for Language learners and teachers, and others. In 2014–15, Steven project managed the creation of the ALL Literature wiki (http://ALL-Literature.wikidot.com) which he continues to maintain and edit.

**Ruth Heilbronn** gained her PhD in philosophy of education at the UCL Institute of Education and has led various teams engaged in teacher education in her work at the institute. She has taught modern foreign languages as a French and Spanish teacher in London secondary schools and been variously head of department, deputy head and LEA advisor. Her publications include research on the induction of newly qualified teachers for the Department for Education (Research Report 338, 2002) and articles and book chapters on ethical teacher education, values education, reflective practice and ethical deliberation. Some of her relevant publications include *Teacher Education and the Development of Practical Judgement* (Continuum, 2008) and co-edited books, *Research-Based Best Practice for Schools* (Routledge, 2002); *Critical Practice in Teacher Education*, with John Yandell (IoE Press, 2010); *Comprehensive Achievements* (Trentham Books, 2014), with Imison and Williams; *Philosophical Perspectives on Teacher Education*, with Lorraine Foreman-Peck (Wiley Blackwell, 2015); *Dewey in Our Time*, with Peter Cunningham (UCL IoE Press, 2016); *Teacher Development 3.0* (TEdX2017 online); and *Dewey and Education in the 21st Century* (Emerald Books, 2018), with Christine Doddington and Rupert Higham. She is an executive member of the Philosophy of Education Society of Great Britain (PESGB). In all her work, she has sought to combat an instrumental approach to teaching.

**Jane Jones** is Head of MFL Teacher Education at King's College London that includes PGCE and MA programmes and associated doctoral studies. She won the KCL Supervisory Excellence Award 2017 for her support of PhD students. Jane was junior-secondary trained and taught MFL in school for sixteen years and has been involved in teacher education for over forty years. She has published widely on teaching, learning, assessment and leadership issues in languages. She is lead author of the bestseller *Modern Foreign Languages 5–11: Issues for Teachers* (2016). Jane has led sixteen EU-funded projects that have enabled her to develop a cross-cultural overview of language classrooms and pedagogies. Her research interests focus on assessment in the languages classroom (see Jones and Wiliam's *Modern Foreign Languages Inside the Black Box* [2008]) and on the transition from primary to secondary language learning (see, for example, Jones's *Transition from Primary to Secondary Language Learning: Using an Assessment for Learning Approach to Unpack Pupils' 'Suitcases of Skills and Abilities'* [2016]).

She is working on a project with school and university colleagues in Paris on independent language learning and on teacher research projects with primary languages teachers and University colleagues in Madrid. She has written about teacher research in her chapter 'Teachers as emergent critical researchers of their practice' in Christie and Conlon's *Success Stories from Secondary FL Classrooms* (2016). She is co-editor of submissions for the initiative of the Association of Language Learning 'Learning from the Classroom' that publishes on the ALL website short scholarly accounts by teachers of their research. Jane is keen to support teachers to become researchers of their practice in a critically engaged community of practice.

**Frances Weightman** is associate professor of Chinese Studies at the University of Leeds. She runs the AHRC-funded 'Writing Chinese' project on contemporary Chinese authors and their works (https://writingchinese.leeds.ac.uk) and is actively engaged in the promotion of new Chinese literature in translation to a broad audience, working in partnership with publishers and teachers, including developing school book clubs, teacher training seminars and translation competitions. In 2014, she was awarded Leeds University's Partnership Award for Inspirational Teaching. She works closely with colleagues in secondary schools and is a passionate believer in the need for more collaboration between the secondary and tertiary sectors. With a PhD from the University of Edinburgh (2002) on seventeenth-century classical Chinese ghost stories, and a former holder of a Leverhulme Trust Special Research Fellowship, she now publishes on both modern and premodern Chinese fiction. She is the author of *The Quest for the Childlike in Seventeenth-Century Chinese Fiction: Fantasy, Naivety, and Folly* (2008); the co-editor (with Anders Hansson and Bonnie S. McDougall) of *The Chinese at Play: Festivals, Games and Leisure* (2002); the co-editor (with Gao Wanlong and Wang Aimin) of *Chinese Cultural Terms and Phrases in English* (2015); and the co-editor (with Sarah Dodd) of *Chinese Journeys*, a special issue of Stand Magazine (2018), on new Chinese writing. She is chair of the Expert Panel for the Department for Education's Mandarin Excellence Programme, co-founder and co-chair of the Association for Speakers of Chinese as a Second Language (www.chinesespeakers.org) and currently represents area studies on the Executive Committee of the University Council for Modern Languages.

# Introduction

*Fotini Diamantidaki*

Many years ago Widdowson (1994) stated, 'You are proficient in a language to the extent that you possess it, make it your own, bend it to your will, assert yourself through it rather than simply submit to the dictates of its form' (384). 'Form' as in lexicon: 'lexical categories' and 'functional categories'. 'Lexical categories' mean words such as verbs, nouns and more 'functional categories' of those words such as tenses and auxiliaries (Mitchell & Myles, 2004: 54). Widdowson's statement has contemporary resonance, especially in challenging transitional times that we live in. It makes me wonder what are the priorities in foreign language teaching, what to teach and if given all curriculum constraints, in any context, whether teachers can go further than just teaching the 'form'.

Within the English context (for which this book has been initiated), the incorporation of literary texts in modern foreign languages (MFLs) is a re-emerging research area, due to the resurgence of literature use in the classroom as dictated by the latest National Curriculum for languages (DfE, 2013a). The study of literary texts seem to feature from key stage 2 (primary school) as part of 'the focus of study in modern languages [ ... ] on practical communication' (DfE KS2, 2013b: 2) with the view of providing 'a linguistic foundation for reading comprehension and an appreciation of [ ... ] civilisation' (DfE KS2, 2013b: 2). 'Appreciate stories, songs, poems and rhymes in the language' (DfE KS2, 2013b: 2) are genres suggested to introduce at primary school level.

At secondary school level, key stage 3 (KS3) (secondary school ages 11–13), learners are expected to 'read literary texts in the language [such as stories, songs, poems and letters] to stimulate ideas, develop creative expression and expand understanding of the language and culture' (DfE KS3, 2013c: 2), building on what they started in primary school and working more specifically on reading skills, using literature as a tool for further creativity and as a means to appreciate the culture of the language taught.

At key stage 4 (secondary school ages 14–16), literature is one of the types of written texts that students are expected to understand: 'students will be expected to understand different types of written language, including relevant personal communication, public information, factual and literary texts, appropriate to this level' (DfE, 2015a: 4) with the suggestion for the choice of texts becoming more elaborate: 'literary texts can include extracts and excerpts, adapted and abridged as appropriate, from poems, letters, short stories, essays, novels or plays from contemporary and historical sources, subject to copyright' (DfE, 2015a: 4).

At key stage 5 (school ages 16–18), what is new is that one literary work at least is to be studied thoroughly with the view to 'analyse' it and 'respond to it critically in writing' (DfE, 2015b: 6). More specifically in point 12 of the statutory document it is stated, 'At A level, students must develop a more detailed understanding of the works, showing a critical appreciation of the concepts and issues covered, and a critical and analytical response to features such as the form and the technique of presentation, as appropriate to the work studied' (DfE, 2015b: 6).

What is striking is that we seem to go around in circles and still keep focusing on 'teaching the form', even at the most advanced stage of schooling. 'Form' is certainly important to consider in relation to accountability and exams. But it shouldn't be the only focus.

Hanauer (2012) states that the language classroom has been to a certain extent 'dehumanised' (105) and that language learning directed by the 'imposition of abstract standards, requirement for particular teaching methods and evaluation tied to external standardised tests' (105) has led to teaching more of the linguistic aspects and structures of the language. 'Thus, the language learner at the center of this system becomes nothing more than an intellectual entity involved in an assessable cognitive process' (105).

Surely, 'simply learning a foreign language is a life changing event for any learner and it should involve the entire human being, beyond than just intellectual abilities' (105).

To this effect, teaching literary texts in the MFL classroom is 'suitable because language is learned by human beings and the interest and love of literature for its various qualities is a human characteristic' (Paran, 2008: 469). Shanahan (1997) supports the idea that 'our fundamental goal as language professionals is to expand and enrich the lives of our students and the society in which they live' (171), by exposing learners to literary texts that can not only reflect the culture of the language studied but also reflecting upon the society the learners live in.

Widdowson (1998) argues that foreign language learning is 'decontextualized' and that 'language can only be made pragmatically real if it is reconnected up with context of some kind' (712). Literature can provide that specific context for the teachers and students who experience it. Widdowson (2003) suggests that it is 'people who make a text real by realising it as discourse, that is to say by relating to specific contexts of communal cultural values and attitudes' (98). In my view, a literary text has the power to involve learners and help them evolve as individuals. It allows learners to look critically at their own cultural values and attitudes and given the opportunity, recreate a new cultural reality (Diamantidaki, 2016). Furthermore, access to literary texts can lead to more creative forms of teaching where the learner is at the centre of the experience and acts and reacts as a human being, reconnecting with the context they are living and the context they are studying, not functioning just as a languages learner at the receiving end of the teaching process.

To this end and with the above framework in mind, the current collection of chapters from esteemed colleagues in the UK and the United States aims to suggest more creative forms of teaching MFLs through literature, in association with developing target language use, drama, poetry, storylines, multimedia, philosophy, teaching in primary, teaching non-roman script languages such as Japanese and Mandarin Chinese. The lack of literature in the field of teaching of literature in MFL has also incited me to organize this publication with the view to start addressing the gap in research.

The collection of chapters, therefore, examines how literary texts can be incorporated into teaching practices in an MFL classroom with the view to enrich teaching practices in a creative way, where learners are at the centre of the teaching process. Each chapter is enriched by three pedagogical features: reflection points with questions for teachers, students and teacher educators, tasks designed for classroom use and research boxes summarizing research in the relevant discipline, a user-friendly approach to access research.

# The content of each chapter

In Chapter 1, Ruth Heilbronn is concerned with the fundamental importance of teaching literature in school. The chapter links two key ideas: the first is the power of 'the narrative imagination', and the second is the way in which education can play a key role in social development and in the development of people who are at home in diverse and democratic societies. The chapter first defines the narrative imagination as the capacity to understand another person's perspective. This matters, because only with this sympathetic understanding can people develop the kinds of openness to others that are required in a democratic society. The chapter then connects the importance of education for democratic citizenship with the ability to reflect and to deliberate. In the development of such critical dispositions, the arts, and particularly literature, have a vital role to play. The reasons why this is the case were pertinently expressed in Dewey's belief that education needs to start in understanding mutual dependency of society and children, in the sense that young people experience and experiment within the social milieu and are also receiving the culture and mediated experience of adults. The chapter discusses Dewey's view of the nature of culture as the sustaining environment that develops habits and dispositions. The capacity for deliberation and reflection is a key to sustaining a democratic disposition and hence a culture in which openness to others is fundamental. Exposure to the life of others, through the narratives found in a variety of literary sources, stimulates the narrative imagination. However, this exposure needs to be accompanied with a classroom experience of discussion in which divergent views are valued and seriously considered. With this in place, a habituating environment can encourage reflection and debate to nourish the imagination, and develop the capacity to talk back to policies and practices which are essential for democratic citizenship.

In Chapter 2, Jane Jones examines foreign language learning in primary school. Much learning in primary languages tends to centre on exposure to vocabulary or very simple sentence structures that often rule out a meaningful engagement with more extended texts and literature. This has traditionally been the preserve of more advanced stages of MFL learning. There have been developments in recent years to consider how young language learners can engage with texts and literature, and this chapter will consider some of the creative practices teachers use. This is explored in the cultural contexts of Germany, Spain and England. After a consideration of what literature means to teachers, the texts and literature children are exposed to in their mother tongue learning environment as well as in their MFL lessons in primary language lessons are identified in a series of vignettes in the three contexts. The teachers' narratives have a central place in this chapter concerning their literature choices and the activities they employ, and their pupils also comment on what they enjoy. Hans Eberhard Piepho's emphasis on the story structure as a linguistically and pedagogically rich means for enabling children's language progression is the theoretical linchpin of the chapter. The chapter concludes that all language learners can obtain considerable benefits and enjoyment from their engagement with texts and literature and that primary language teachers can readily embed these into their programmes.

In Chapter 3, Jennifer Eddy examines a performance assessment design model that unfolds literary works through three modes of communication, interpretive, interpersonal and presentational, with current and practical approaches to teaching about and through drama. Questions such as the following are addressed during the chapter: how do we know when the learner truly understands? To what extent does creativity, drama and novelty play a role in task design for understanding literature? What does transfer look like? When the learner achieves transfer, they can use knowledge and skills differently than how they were originally taught to create something new. Artists, composers and authors do this all the time; Jennifer Eddy advocates that our students can too, by looking at task design that encourages creativity and critical thinking skills as learners, transform one work of art into another. Learners will understand that literature can inspire other genres. This helps learners see that literature is not fixed or static and that they can also create something new. This moves the learner forward and beyond rote facts about the content towards integration of language, culture and content. Pedagogical features include reflection questions, sample performance tasks, can-do statements for learner engagement, accountability and implementation, and a template for creating the performance assessment. These tasks encourage flexibility, tolerance of ambiguity and autonomy, all key characteristics of intercultural competence. By transforming these works of art, these novel tasks effectively shorten the creative distance between the artist and learner.

In Chapter 4, Verna Brandford examines the Storyline approach. Storylines are simulations with narrative structures and can be cross-curricular. The Storyline approach can be used with any phase, including with adults. While one immediately thinks of the reading skill when considering the inclusion of stories in the curriculum, the chapter starts from the premise that we all communicate, think and learn through stories. Stories can come in a wide variety of forms ranging from personal experiences, anecdotes and jokes to adaptations of well-known works of literature and texts. The Storyline approach and its components are defined within the sociocultural and co-constructive narrative paradigms which underpin it drawing particularly on the work of Jerome Bruner and Lev Vygotsky. Both theorists suggest that by creating a dialogic teaching and learning environment where the pupils share and discuss their understanding and make sense of the world, they can also be motivated and benefit from pedagogy that encourages them to collaborate, make decisions and choices as they demonstrate their learning in different ways and through different skills. The chapter explores how the flexibility of the approach affords the language teacher and learner a number of significant opportunities to exploit literary texts in meaningful and creative ways, simultaneously facilitate the teaching and practice of new subject matter as well as revisit and build on previous learning in new contexts. A Storyline pedagogic approach is posited and exemplified through the use of the extract 'La pluie' from the book *Le petit Nicolas et les copains* by Sempé/Goscinny (1963).

In Chapter 5, Frances Weightman examines the Chinese teaching in UK schools which gradually shifts from 'textbook' dialogues to an emphasis on the study of literary texts. Chinese is a challenging enough language for Europeans to learn well, with its non-phonetic script and a fundamentally different grammatical system. It takes many more hours of dedicated study for our students to become proficient in Chinese as a second language than in, say, French or German, and this is particularly true for their reading and writing skills. Despite huge advances in language learning software and pedagogy, there simply is no magic shortcut to avoid the memorization of thousands of characters. The prospect of incorporating the study of Chinese literature into an already tight secondary school MFL curriculum is therefore understandably daunting for teachers. Chinese teaching in UK schools received a significant boost, with the arrival of the Mandarin Excellence Programme, providing intensive teaching of Chinese language in selected schools on the programme, while aiming for the study of Chinese language and culture to become increasingly embedded across the secondary curriculum. At the same time, in line with the new National Curriculum for all MFL teaching, the nature of what is taught is also shifting away from 'textbook' dialogues, with new emphasis on the study of literary texts. Insisting that the syllabus for Chinese mirrors that for European languages, despite the considerable linguistic differences, is a cause for concern for many teachers. Literature, for these teachers, whether Chinese nationals or UK-trained, is often taken to mean the great classical works – and how can these be adequately abridged or simplified to an appropriate level of language for the pupils they teach? In this chapter, there is the suggestion that the linguistic complexities of Chinese may in fact strengthen the rationale for inclusion of some literary texts in the Chinese language teaching curriculum, aiding motivation and providing opportunities for deeper reflection and cross-cultural understanding to complement rote memorization and ultimately lead to a more stimulating, and meaningful, approach to the study of Chinese.

In Chapter 6, I focus on the teaching of poetry in the French foreign language classroom as part of a MFL lesson. With the introduction of the new national curriculum and the suggestion to integrate literary texts in the process of teaching including poems, the chapter demonstrates how poems can be incorporated within the teaching process, in order to promote not only vocabulary awareness, listening, speaking and reading and writing skills, but also creative personal interpretation. The aim of the chapter is to demonstrate that poetry is not for the elite readers and that the earlier the reading of poems are introduced to young learners, the more chances there are to appreciate the language and its culture in the longer run. A plethora of paradigms in French and how to explore them will provide teachers with a bank of ideas to introduce and explore poetry within the linguistic topics that need teaching.

In Chapter 7, Colin Christie discusses the use of the target language (TL). Its use by students at key stages 3 and 4, he argues, is often limited to more transactional, topic-based exchanges. This can mean that talking about more abstract matters is particularly challenging for the teacher to implement. As a result, it is often felt that students do not have the capacity to express themselves in respect to an appreciation of literature as this would require the use of more complex and nuanced language. The chapter shows that students can be taught to talk about literature in the TL, but that this will mean investing time in teaching them the language needed for this purpose. It is language which needs to be practised and developed over time, demanding patience and constant revisiting on the part of the teacher. This will lead to a repertoire of set phrases which can be used as they stand but also adapted as necessary. The chapter will also demonstrate how students can be motivated to engage with texts in a way which incentivizes them to speak in the TL. With the new requirement at 'A' level for students to write about literature in the TL, it will again be shown how such an ability can be built up incrementally. Students should not be expected to simply write at length in the TL on demand. They need to be involved in different TL activities in the course of reading and discussing texts over time. Examples of these will be presented and discussed.

In Chapter 8, Steven Fawkes discusses the creation of the Association of Language Learning (ALL) literature wiki as a reaction to the newest version of the National Curriculum for England; when introduced, or refocused on several elements, language teachers found quite a change from the existing curriculum requirements. These include a focus on translation, on grammar, on spontaneous speaking and in the integration of literature into the teaching scheme of work. It was in response to this last concern that ALL volunteers identified the need to support colleagues in very practical ways. The chapter initially describes the process of creating the wiki (http://ALL-Literature.wikidot.com), which involved several challenges: discussing what sort of texts should be included, researching documentation and resources to populate different area of the wiki, mobilizing contributions from members of ALL through a range of strategies, forming a steering group to devise the templates, and design the wiki interfaces, ongoing maintenance and stimulation of further contributions. The chapter also compares approaches suggested by contributors, including some international aspects, and explores in some detail the sorts of interaction that teachers consider appropriate when language learners are interacting with authentic texts, in order to cover the multiple objectives they are planning for: coping with authenticity, expanding vocabulary, developing linguistic skills such as listening for detail or speaking with confidence, exploring grammar in a context, stimulating creative use of language, learning about sound/spelling conventions, the place of translating and interpreting as well as the eternal challenge of motivation. The chapter concludes by suggesting a number of strategies that can be applied to texts of different sorts, with examples from the wiki itself.

# References

DfE. (2013a). 'National Curriculum in England: Languages Programmes of Study'. Accessed April 2018 from https://www.gov.uk/government/publications/national-curriculum-in-england-languages-progammes-of-study/national-curriculum-in-england-languages-progammes-of-study.

DfE. (2013b). 'Languages Programmes of Study: Key stage 2, National curriculum in England'. Accessed November 2017 from https://www.gov.uk/government/uploads/system/uploads/attachment_data/file/239042/PRIMARY_national_curriculum_-_Languages.pdf.

DfE. (2013c). 'Languages Programmes of Study: Key Stage 3 National Curriculum in England'. Accessed November 2017 from https://www.gov.uk/government/uploads/system/uploads/attachment_data/file/239083/SECONDARY_national_curriculum_-_Languages.pdf.

DfE. (2015a). 'Modern Foreign Languages, GCSE Subject Content'. Accessed November 2017 from https://www.gov.uk/government/uploads/system/uploads/attachment_data/file/485567/GCSE_subject_content_modern_foreign_langs.pdf.

DfE. (2015b). 'Modern Foreign Languages, GCE AS and A level Subject Content'. Accessed April 2018 from https://assets.publishing.service.gov.uk/government/uploads/system/uploads/attachment_data/file/485569/GCE_A_AS_level_subject_content_modern_foreign_langs.pdf.

Diamantidaki, F. (2016). 'Using Literature in the KS3 Foreign Language Classroom'. In C. Conlon (Ed.), *Success Stories from Secondary Foreign Languages Classrooms: Models from London School Partnerships with Universities*. London: Trentham.

Hanauer, D. (2012). 'Meaningful Literacy: Writing Poetry in the Language Classroom'. *Language Teaching*, 45(1): 105–15. doi:10.1017/S0261444810000522.

Mitchell, R. and F. Myles. (2004). *Second Language Learning Theories*, 2nd ed. London: Hodder Arnold.

Paran, A. (2008). 'The Role of Literature in Instructed Foreign Language Learning and Teaching: An Evidence-Based Survey'. *Language Teaching*, 41(4): 465–96. doi:10.1017/S026144480800520X.

Sempé, G. (1963). *Le petit Nicolas et les copains*. Editions Folio Junior.

Shanahan, D. (1997). 'Articulating the Relationship between Language, Literature, and Culture: Toward a New Agenda for Foreign Language Teaching and Research'. *Modern Language Journal*, 81: 164–74. doi:10.1111/j.1540–4781.1997.tb01171.x.

Widdowson, H. G. (1994). 'The Ownership of English'. *TESOL Quarterly*, 28: 377–89. doi:10.2307/3587438.

Widdowson, H. G. (1998). 'Context, Community, and Authentic Language'. *TESOL Quarterly*, 32: 705–16. doi:10.2307/3588001.

Widdowson, H. G. (2003). *Defining Issues in English Language Teaching*. Oxford: Oxford University Press.

# 1

# Literature, Culture and Democratic Citizenship

*Ruth Heilbronn*

## Introduction

This chapter is about the fundamental importance of teaching literature in school, and in discussing this I draw particularly on ideas elaborated by Martha Nussbaum and John Dewey to explore how the teaching of literature contributes to the development of 'narrative imagination', the capacity to understand another person's perspective, and how discussing characters' interactions and dilemmas helps students to engage with social and interpersonal ethical issues.

In education systems worldwide, there is a premium on a 'knowledge-based curriculum', that is one in which students study subjects believed to give them the knowledge and skills needed for employment in twenty-first-century conditions. This is primarily an economic aim for education, with the curriculum generally focused on subjects thought useful to give 'transferable skills and knowledge'. Subjects in the curriculum which are given importance in terms of curriculum time are those related to employability and to the idea of a global economy and global economic competition. These are mainly the STEM subjects (Science, Technology, Engineering and Mathematics) with English often coming to be defined as literacy and with some limited time for humanities, the creative arts and languages, and this particularly impacts on the place of literature in the modern foreign language (MFL) classroom. The mechanism of competition, between schools and ultimately between countries, is used to provide the evidence required that the nation's education system is effective or not. 'Effectiveness' is a key aim in this paradigm of what education should be, and effectiveness is defined in terms of quantitative data, such as examination results, which becomes the 'evidence base' for 'effectiveness' and is then used to drive education policy and curricular choices.

Necessarily in an educational culture in which assessment drives the curriculum, what is studied in school will be heavily managed to provide the evidence for the auditing of results. Performance management of teachers is one of the ways in which teachers are routinely monitored to ensure that they 'deliver' results (Isaac Mwita, 2000; Gleeson & Husbands, 2004). The culture which drives this activity has been described and analysed as a performativity culture (Davies, 2003; Ball, 2012; Murray, 2012). In education, professionals are tasked to rely on procedures to regulate their practices and since grades in examinations are the desired outcome in this scenario, an understandable tendency to 'teach to the test' often leads to a narrowing of the kinds of approaches to teaching so that what are perceived as 'safe' methods are the norm. This can lead to prescribing a specific kind of pedagogy, such as how to teach language in single words, chunks or language functions, and also in curriculum planning to accommodate demands of a specific pedagogy, as was common in MFL teaching in 1970s and 1980s. Then a communicative methodology with total use of target language was dominant, opposing an earlier mode of grammar-translation as the fundamental MFL teaching methodology. In non-MFL subjects, this trend towards prescribing a specific curriculum can be seen in history, for example, in a view that key events or dates signifying a 'nation's history' should be the basis of study. In literature teaching in MFL as well as in English, this can be seen when canonical texts are recommended.

In a system judged by performance measurements, assessment ends tend to drive curricula and pedagogy. Some critics, such as Diane Ravitch, warn against excessive testing and audit in education:

> It behoves us to take seriously concerns that the current emphasis on testing and inspection distorts the purposes of education. We no longer speak of education as a process of human development. (Ravitch, 2013: 265)

If we focus on language as the medium through which human development, in the form of culture, is enacted, we might argue that this distortion occurs when we separate teaching and learning into four discrete skill areas and test these separately. Discourse cannot be disaggregated in this way.

## Reflection 1

*Technicist and technical rationality*

Writers use different terms for the kind of educational practice that is based on narrow goals of education, such as is exemplified in an economic model or one in which there is thought to be a 'science of teaching' that can be laid out using evidence about 'what works'. This kind of view of practice is based on a view termed 'technical rational', following Dewey and also the philosopher Habermas who described 'instrumental rationality' in management. Technicist approaches assume that what needs to be managed; the purposes to be achieved, and the management process, are clear, fixed and unproblematic, whereas 'real life' is not actually that clear-cut.

What do you understand by a technically rational approach to learning?

- Can you give examples of practices that fit this definition, in your experience?
- Where might such an approach be effective and useful?
- Where might it not be adequate?

# What is education for?

The model of education which is based primarily on effectiveness in examinations and league tables is only one way of underpinning educational policies and practices. Rather than starting from the auditing of achievement in examinations as the fundamental aim of education, we could start with a different primary aim. We could ask which human qualities and capabilities we wish to nurture and what kind of society we hope for. We could then ask, as did the philosopher Michael Oakeshott in the 1970s, questions like the following: what is the character of the world which a human newcomer is to inhabit? What does it mean to become human? Which human qualities do we wish to nurture and develop and how could education foster them? (Oakeshott, 1972). If we start from this more flexible proposition, rather than the economic aim, schools, curriculum and the work of teachers would look different from the current model. Richard Pring calls this 'learning to be human', which involves

> first the acquisitions of knowledge and understanding to help one manage life intelligently; practical capabilities, and a developed sense of community with which our own well-being is connected … Most importantly added to this is the moral dimension in which young persons are enabled to see life as a whole, to think seriously about the life worth living, to recognise excellence and to want to pursue it in the activities they are engaged in. (Pring, 2012: 32)

Engagement with this moral dimension is also an aim of education, that is, to foster a sense of 'moral seriousness'.

## Reflection 2

*Humanistic aims of education*

1 Do you agree that basing education on the humanistic aims discussed by Oakeshott and Pring requires that teachers develop the dispositions to be open and welcoming to the possibility of ambiguity and complexity?
2 What is the role of teacher judgement? Is being able to exercise judgement important to your view of your role of a teacher?
3 What do you understand by the term 'managerial teacher' or 'technician of education', and how do questions 2 and 3 relate to question 1?
4 What kind of role might be played in this respect when students and teachers together tackle literary texts?
5 What kind of quality is 'moral seriousness' for you? Is it important for you as a teacher to support its development for your students?

# Education as a social process

An argument is often put forward that literature should be taught in the foreign language classroom because it introduces children to the culture represented in that language. But there is also a more fundamental reason for why literature matters, and this is related to the quality of 'moral seriousness'. Before going on to discuss literature teaching specifically, this section discusses the social basis of education and educational development. The quality of moral seriousness which we hope to foster in education matters because human development is a social process. From the time they are born, babies develop a sense of the meanings of things by interacting with others, who understand the baby's gestures as communicative. The feedback given to the baby develops a meaning for gestures and at a later stage, language (Mead, 1934: 76, 81; Quarantelli & Cooper, 1966; McCall, 1977). As Elliot (1981) has shown, the young child who is learning language in interaction with others is also developing on all fronts, not just the linguistic one, and is trying to make sense of her social environment and the world of objects around her as well as what is coming at her as linguistic input.

So children are not isolated individuals and in this respect, John Dewey's comment is as pertinent today as when he wrote it, over a hundred years ago. He reminds us that

> only as we interpret school activities with reference to the larger circle of social activities to which they relate do we find any standard for judging their moral significance. (Dewey, 1909: 13)

He argued that the school is a place with a fundamental moral purpose relating to inducting children into the life of society and preparing them to take their place in the world. To accept the moral purpose of the school and the school as a place where children are together in what he called 'a form of associated living' presupposes interacting with people on the basis of mutuality and this means that whether it is explicitly stated or not, 'the moral purpose of the school is universal and dominant in all instruction, whatever the topic' (Dewey, 1909: 2). The school's role is 'the development of character through all the agencies, instrumentalities and materials of school life' (3). Dewey believes that the child acquires a moral sense through learning in all subjects in which she is experimenting or actively engaged with ideas and 'the school is an institution erected by society to contribute to maintaining the life and advancing the welfare of society' (7). Crucially, 'we must take the child as a member of society in the broadest sense, and demand for and from the schools whatever is necessary to enable the child intelligently to recognize all his social relations and take his part in sustaining them' (8), while enabling the child's individual development. The child is 'an organic whole, intellectually, socially and morally, as well as physically' (11). This rich view of the child to be educated entails an ethical responsibility on the school to provide an education which will give the child 'such possession of himself that he may take charge of himself' and in so doing 'have power to shape and direct social changes' (Dewey, 1909). How can literature help in this process?

# Why teach literature

So far the chapter has put forward a view of education as a social undertaking and the idea of a humanistic education as one which develops students' capabilities and capacities for positive social engagement as well as educating them for their own development and individual achievements. Students studying literature have commented on its importance throughout their studies, and this applies particularly to the MFL classroom. They have talked about 'the power in stories'; the way in which 'we can capture and interpret what has happened and is happening to us personally and to the world as a whole' and how this helps understanding that one is truly part of human society; and helps understanding in 'what it means to live in the world', because it can 'provide insights that cold hard facts do not'.[1]

Martha Nussbaum (1996a, 1996b, 1996c) is a classical scholar and moral philosopher who argues that through literature we can develop empathy and 'moral imagination' which is the capacity to more fully put ourselves in another person's situation. When we do this, it is less likely that we will view others as different, or dehumanized and 'Other-ised' (Bromwich, 1996). Moral imagination is a source of this 'moral seriousness' that enables us to empathize with others and relate to others as engaged in our common humanity. Literature is important in foreign language teaching in the process of becoming a morally serious person. Since education is a social undertaking, education for humanistic aims seeks to develop students' capabilities and capacities for social engagement as well as their own individual development. Again Dewey points the way to why this is important when he says that we lose much of the value of literature and language studies if we do not emphasize the social element. Language, he reminds us,

> is fundamentally and primarily a social instrument. Language is the device for communication; it is the tool through which one individual comes to share the ideas and feelings of others. When treated simply as a way of getting individual information, or as a means of showing off what one has learned, it loses its social motive and end. (Dewey, 1897)

As Nussbaum argues, literature is a way to nourish human needs because it expands our empathy and develops our moral imagination. Through encouraging us to exercise moral imagination, we can cultivate the capacity to put ourselves in another person's situation. Through engaging with characters' lives in a novel or play, for example, we gain an insight into their experiences. When we connect with narratives of characters, it is because we recognize their feelings and perceive their responses to circumstances. When we do react to characters and narratives in this way, we experience the humanity of others. This puts us in touch with a common humanity: it bridges gaps between those 'different' to ourselves. So, sympathy in this sense is a vital part of a moral imagination because it helps us to regard others as fundamentally like ourselves, rather than strange, alien, other.

When we use literary texts in MFL, we frequently encounter examples of the power of literature to speak to the moral imagination beyond the culture in which the work was formed, for example, the late twentieth-century feminist reading of Tolstoy's *Anna Karenina* (Armstrong, 1988; Evans, 1988; Heldt, 1992; Mandelker, 1993); or the place of women as depicted by Molière (Tebben, 1999); or Lorca's attitude towards the women in his plays (Johnson, 2008 – see also Marks, 1978; and Moi, 2008), particularly writing on Nathalie Sarraute.

When literature is taught in the languages classroom inevitably discussion is needed to gain understanding of the text. Some cultural references might be transmitted didactically but for students to understand a text they need to engage interactively with it and with each other.

This itself is an important reason for teaching literature. Discussion and debate is crucial to developing a critically alert sense and therefore essential in education. More than this, the kinds of situations and dilemmas that students encounter through the lives of the characters in plays and novels are often one of moral ambiguity and in considering these situations together students are engaging in 'a dramatic rehearsal (in imagination) of various competing lines of action' (Dewey, 1922: 132).

> Deliberation is an experiment in finding out what the various lines of possible action are really like ... to see what the resultant action would be like if it were entered upon. But the trial is in imagination, not in overt fact... An act overtly tried out is irrevocable, its consequences cannot be blotted out. An act tried out in imagination is not final or fatal. It is retrievable. (Dewey, 1922: 133)

Engaging in deliberation of this kind, at one remove from people's personal life situations, enables a distance from important issues that need to be aired. An example is Camus's 1947 novel which is written about a plague in Oran but was an extended metaphor for the occupation of France from 1940 to 1945. It raises many ethical issues and the book is about courage, the sense of social responsibility and even heroism, human characteristics such as meanness and generosity, 'about small heroism and large cowardice, and about all kinds of profoundly humanist problems, such as love and goodness, happiness and mutual connection' (Warner, 2003).

In fact, literary examples are used as illustrations and cases in moral philosophy as they can provide more complex descriptions of moral dilemmas and problems of practical reasoning than examples generated from rules or schema devised for the purpose of testing rules.

> By 'more complex' we usually mean either that they better reflect the real social and psychological conditions under which we make moral decisions or could plausibly imagine making them, or that – even if the literary scenario is implausible under current social conditions (say, a passage of science fiction describing brain transplantation) – such examples will assist deep reflection on morals and morality. (Small, 2013)

## Reflective activity 1

*Your own response to literature*

1  Do you read fiction? Or go to the theatre? If so, can you say something about this? If you do not, why do you think fiction does not appeal to you? Do you read other kinds of books or poetry?
2  Do you perhaps write yourself in any way, such as a journal or a blog? If so, who do you write for? Do your readers matter?
3  In novels or plays that you have read or seen, is there a character or characters with whom you have sympathized or felt particularly close? Why? Any other reflection?

# Reflective activity 2

*Choosing texts for teaching*

**1** Which texts might you use in your teaching to stimulate discussion on moral issues?

**2** Finding texts at A level is usually easier than at KS4 and KS3. Are there any texts that you know of that might be useful for younger students, such as fables and folk tales?

N.B. It is worth exploring websites for your target language to find suitable texts. For readers in KS3 and KS4, there are sites related to stories studied in the later years of primary school in the target language countries, and teachers in this phase of education may have useful suggestions for work on those texts. The prose is directed to primary-age children, and it is often possible to choose a text which is of interest to secondary school students in KS3 or even KS4 that has a language level which is more accessible than a text whose primary target language audience is adults. Daniel Pennac's *L'oeil du Loup* is an example for the French class, which can tap into the universal appeal of 'narrative sympathy' and 'moral imagination'. A further example is *Voyage au Pays des Arbres* by J. M. G. Le Clezio.[2]

## Task for teachers to try in the classroom

*L'oeil du loup*, Daniel Pennac – (Editions Pocket Junior, 2009)

This book is studied in primary schools in France and it is worth studying in KS4, or even KS3 with some classes, because the text is easy to understand with help, but the book itself is complex – both in its narrative structure, with flashbacks to the experiences of the two protagonists, with two different viewpoints – and raises important questions about human emotion, loneliness and the relations between children and animals. There are many worksheets and schemes of work in French on the internet, for example, the following lesson has been written by Suzy Malzieu and Collette Raussac and is freely available at http://ressources.crdp-aquitaine.fr/attirelireV2/viewDocument.aspx?niv=8&doc=108&rub=2142.

Hopefully there will be time to study the book further and use the further resources posted.

## Objectifs

- Dégager les données importantes qui permettront de mieux comprendre
- Étudier de manière précise un passage essentiel pour le sens et la forme

## Déroulement

### 1 – Questions sur la situation initiale

- Le titre du chapitre est: « leur rencontre », de qui parle-t-on?
- Où cela se passe-t-il? Quels sont les mots dans ce chapitre qui situent le lieu avec précision?
- Quelle est l'attitude du loup vis-à-vis des hommes? Quelle en est la raison?
- Quelle est son attitude vis-à-vis du garçon? Comment évolue-t-elle?

*2 – Sur les pages 5, 7 et 8*

Il est bon de faire un travail précis sur les substituts (pronoms personnels) ce qui permet d'affiner la compréhension.

Faire prendre conscience aux élèves que dans ce passage le narrateur est extérieur, que l'on a uniquement le point de vue du loup et que les paroles sont l'expression de sa pensée.

*3 – Étude particulière d'un passage pages 12–13: « Il n'y a que ce garçon ... le temps devant eux. »*

- Relecture du passage silencieusement
- Lecture à haute voix par l'enseignant (dramatiser pour faire ressentir l'atmosphère, sa tension puis sa poésie)

*- Questions*

a   Qu'est-ce qui gène le loup? Faire retrouver le passage et le faire relire par un élève.

b   « *Pour rien au monde il ne détournerait la tête* » Comment expliquer cette phrase? Est-ce qu'on a déjà eu des informations sur cet aspect du caractère du loup? Rechercher et lire dans ce chapitre.

c   « *Ce n'est pas du chagrin, c'est de l'impuissance et de la colère* » Pourquoi de l'impuissance et de la colère?

d   Tout à coup le climat de la scène change. Comment? Quel mot le traduit?

e   « *... avec tout le temps devant eux* » Qu'est-ce qui se noue à partir de ce moment? Comment pensez-vous que la situation va évoluer? Que pourra peut-être lui apporter ce garçon?

*Objectives*

- Identify important elements that will lead to a better understanding.
- Study a typical passage for meaning and style.

*1 – Questions about the initial situation*

- The title of the chapter is 'their meeting'; who are the people meeting?
- Where does the meeting take place? What words tell you exactly what the place is?
- What is the attitude of the wolf towards people? What is the reason for this attitude?
- What is his attitude towards the boy? How is it developing?

*2 – On pages 5, 7 and 8*

It is advisable to work specifically on the personal pronouns which allow a more refined comprehension.

Make students aware that in this passage the narrator is outside, that we only have the point of view of the wolf and that the words are the expression of his thought.

*3 – Study of a passage on pages 12–13: 'There is only this boy ... the time before them.'*

- Silent individual reading.
- Reading aloud by the teacher (dramatized to feel the atmosphere, its tension then its poetry)

*Questions*

  **1** What's wrong with the wolf? Find the passage and have it re-read by a student.
  **2** 'Nothing could make him turn his head.' How to explain this sentence? Have we had any information about this aspect of the wolf's character? Study the relevant text in this chapter.
  **3** 'It is not sorrow, it is helplessness and anger.' Why does the wolf experience helplessness and anger?
  **4** Suddenly the atmosphere of the scene changes. How? What word conveys it?
  **5** '… with all the time before them'. What is happening from this moment? How do you think the situation will evolve? What can this boy possibly bring the wolf?

Further work on this book can also be found at http://www.i-profs.fr/fiches_pedagogiques/oeilduloup.pdf.

# Literature and democratic citizenship

Literature is important in enabling the development of moral imagination. Classroom discussion on issues raised in the literature read is important to support students in developing their understanding of complex and multifaceted matters. For example, Beaumarchais's play, 'Le Barbier de Seville', features as hero a servant, Figaro. Through watching or reading the play we come to understand that the servant is more clever than his aristocratic master. Questions are raised about why this might have been radical at the time of writing, before the French revolution. Or Maupassant's story 'Les Deux Amis' raises questions about the role of friendship and innocence in a time of war, or the example from Camus's *La Peste*, mentioned earlier. Classroom explorations of this kind enable a safe space for unravelling possible implications of thought and action, for hearing the views of others and for experiencing the reactions of others. Such a mind frame is important to the cultivation of a democratic and inclusive culture.

There are many voices to endorse this view of education. For example, the Council for Europe is concerned that 'in Europe young people do not often have an opportunity to discuss controversial issues in school because they are seen as too challenging to teach'. They point out that lack of opportunities to engage in such discussions can be dangerous:

> Unable to voice their concerns, unaware of how others feel or left to rely on friends and social media for their information, young people can be frustrated or confused about some of the major issues which affect their communities and European society today. In the absence of help from school, they might have no reliable means of dealing with these issues constructively and no one to guide them. (Council of Europe, 2015: 11)

Directly addressing responses to the radicalization of young people, the publication goes on to state,

> Public concern arising in the aftermath of a number of high-profile incidents of violence and social disorder in different European countries has combined with new thinking in education for

democracy and human rights to make the handling of controversial issues in schools a matter of educational urgency. (Council of Europe, 2015)

The Council approves a shift in European policy on education for democracy and human rights 'from reliance on text-book exercises and the acquisition of theoretical knowledge to an emphasis on active and participatory learning and engagement with "real-life" issues' (Council of Europe, 2015).

Nussbaum has argued forcefully not only for the importance of literature but also for the humanities in general (Nussbaum, 2010). As she says,

> Schools that help young people to speak in their own voice and to respect the voices of others will have done a great deal to produce thoughtful and potentially creative democratic citizens.

Teachers have an educative role to play in managing discussions where the curriculum affords opportunities. It is noteworthy how much the humanities and literature teaching can play a role in fostering dialogical pedagogy.

## Window of Research

Johnson, B. (1982). 'Teaching Ignorance: L'Ecole des Femmes'. *Yale French Studies*, 63: 165–82.

Choosing a text that has relevance for students is a key to involving them emotionally and cognitively, which has to happen if students are to engage in deep learning that goes beyond mere familiarity with the studied text. Molière's *L'Ecole des Femmes* is a good choice in this regard because of its subject matter of young people in opposition to their families, outwitting them through age-old means. As Johnson tells us, it is engaging as 'a play about adult authority and adolescent sexuality' (171). Johnson's article stimulates thought on the question of what we should teach, through the provocative title – 'Teaching ignorance'. Provocative because the notion of 'teaching', so often coupled with 'learning', seems contradictory to the idea of 'ignorance' and teaching ignorance

> may, indeed, be a structurally impossible task. For how can a teacher teach a student not to know, without at the same time informing him of what it is he is supposed to be ignorant of? This, at any rate, is the problem faced by the would-be Professor, Arnolphe, in Molière's play *L'Ecole des Femmes*. (Johnson, 1982: 165)

The article first provides the back story to the central characters of Agnes and her guardian Arnolphe, who adopted her when she was four years old and brought her up in seclusion so as to marry her when she comes of age. Arnolphe's teaching method is one of attempting to keep his ward in ignorance so that he may impose his own instruction on what she should do and believe. Arnolphe's intentions are foiled through the love of Agnes and Horace, her young suitor. We learn that Arnolphe's 'negative pedagogy' has not worked: 'his methods are unsound, his lessons backfire, and his classroom is, at the end of the play. silent and empty' (Johnson, 1982: 166).

Today's students would not be as shocked as Molière's contemporaries by the sexual innuendo in the comedy but would likely warm to Arnolphe's problem, as one

> faced by every parent: it is always either too soon or too late to teach children about sexuality. When the play begins, Arnolphe has been handling Agnes' sex education simply by attempting to insure that no learning will take place. (Johnson, 1982: 169)

The article next discusses 'the institutionalization of ignorance' in the play, and this raises an implied question about what we should teach and why. In attempting to control Agnes, Arnolphe gives her a book, Maxims, *On the Duties of the Married Woman*, which is full of interdictions. These lay out that a married woman

> belongs to no one but her husband; she should dress up only for him, receive no visitors but his, accept presents from no man, and never seek to do any writing, to join any feminine social circles, to visit the gambling table, or to go out on walks or picnics. In short, the book for the first time replaces the absence of teaching with the active teaching of the content of ignorance. In place of her former lack of knowledge, the pupil now possesses a knowledge of what she is not supposed to know. (Johnson, 1982: 171)

Unsurprisingly, since the content has now informed Agnes of matters of which she was previously ignorant, Arnolphe's action backfires spectacularly as the play progresses. Johnson asks the interesting questions:

> Could it be that the pedagogical enterprise as such is always constitutively a project of teaching ignorance? Are our ways of teaching students to ask some questions always correlative with our ways of teaching them not to ask-indeed, to be unconscious of-others? Does the educational system exist in order to promulgate knowledge, or is its main function rather to universalize a society's tacit agreement about what it has decided it does not and cannot know? (Johnson, 1982: 173)

This returns us to the issue of why should we choose a literary text in the language classroom and what we might avoid. Will our choice be from a prescribed list? Who has chosen the texts and on what grounds? This again raises a question about bias in an education system and might prompt us to ask what we want to promote as language teachers and more profoundly what knowledge is and how is it transferred. Here we might make a connection with current educational debates in the UK around curricular and engage with the question about decoupling 'knowledge' from its context, such as in teaching communicative chunks of language drawn from daily, interactive situations, rather than tackling a literary text through which language may 'emerge'.

The fourth section of the article explores the theme of Molière's 'feminism' and the interconnection between education and feminism in the seventeenth century. Feminism as a live issue in the twenty-first century evidently provides a powerful factor on student engagement with Molière's text. The section concludes by reminding us that 'the play consistently undercuts the ideology to which it nevertheless still adheres' and then asks, 'Can literature somehow escape or transform power structures by simultaneously espousing and subverting them?' (Johnson, 1982: 176). This is a power of literature, if not to transform lives, at least to alert us to the lives of others, and in this case, the mistakes of others, through the personification and excesses presented.

The fifth section of the article is in some sense the most interesting part of the analysis. It concerns how Agnes learns and what we learn from her about teaching. She recounts her first meeting with Horace.

J'étais sur le balcon à travailler au frais:
Lorsque je vis passer sous les arbres d'auprès
Un jeune homme bien fait, qui rencontrant ma vue,
D'une humble révérence aussitôt me salue.
Moi, pour ne point manquer à la civilité,
Je fis la révérence aussi de mon côté.
Soudain, il me refait une autre révérence.
Moi, j'en refais de même une autre en diligence;
Et lui d'une troisième aussitôt repartant,
D'une troisième aussi j'y repars à l'instant.
Il passe, vient, repasse, et toujours de plus belle
Me fait à chaque fois révérence nouvelle.
Et moi, qui tous ces tours fixement regardais,
Nouvelle révérence aussi je lui rendais.
Tant, que si sur ce point la nuit ne fût venue,
Toujours comme cela je me serais tenue.
Ne voulant point céder et recevoir l'ennui,
Qu'il me pût estimer moins civile que lui.

The significance of Agnes's innocent reciting of the meeting illustrates the core of differences in pedagogy. As Agnes recounts her first meeting with Horace and the beginning of her love for him, she reveals elements we have discussed in the earlier part of the chapter. She recounts an experience that has engaged her, in a setting that is congenial to learning ('au frais', and not confined), in interaction with another who demonstrates sympathetic attachment and who engages her in acting and further experiencing.

As Johnson states,

If Arnolphe is a teacher of the 'do as I say' school, Horace clearly belongs to the school of 'do as I do.' This opposition between the didactic and the mimetic is in fact the classical polarity into which teaching methods can be divided. (1982: 177)

For an MFL teacher, what might alternative teaching modes be? The question is one of keeping alert to the choice between complying with prescriptive and reductive teaching modes, or allowing a space for imagination and development of sentiment through literature. Arnolphe here represents the transmission mode of teaching, whereas through the character of Agnes and her growing awareness of her adult feelings, we have an example of learning through experience.

The article quotes Agnes's letter from the play in French and English (Johnson, 1982: 178–9). It is the only prose section in the play and worth reading. In the light of how she has been shielded from knowledge of the world, the letter is a sophisticated statement about her feelings, and her doubts, arising from her experience of meeting Horace. The experience is what she is analysing and her own ignorance of worldly matters. In itself this text could be taken as an example of the superiority of teaching methods that are rooted in student experience, with all that this implies for respect the individuality of the students. Agnes's letter illustrates the learning that can come about from exposure to experiences which are fruitfully reflected upon. It is Agnes's interrogation of her experiences, both of learning and of her encounter with feelings of love, that win the debate about teaching methods. We can extrapolate from her case the educative power of exposure to 'authentic sources' and how, in combination with non-prescriptive teaching methods, such sources can contribute to students developing the sympathetic imagination discussed at the beginning of this chapter.

Johnson's final thought underscores the point made in this chapter about the importance of teaching literature (182). She develops a term 'positive ignorance', which she defines as 'the pursuit of what is forever in the act of escaping, the inhabiting of that space where knowledge becomes the obstacle to knowing'. This brings us back to the idea at the beginning of the chapter that through literary texts we are in touch with the ambiguity of the lived experience and hence stimulated into developing moral imagination and sympathy.

# Conclusion

This chapter connects the importance of education for democratic citizenship with the ability to reflect and to deliberate and discusses why the arts, and particularly literature, have a vital role to play in this educative process. Teaching literature in the foreign language classroom gives students an opportunity to engage with the culture that has produced the work, and this itself is educative. More than this, through interacting with texts students can come to develop a 'narrative sympathy' that may enable them to engage humanistically with others. Through discussing events, ideas and characters' actions and motivation, students enter a world of moral ambiguity that, paradoxically in a discussion about fiction, is actually a real-life experience of ambiguity. Literature matters and teaching it is important because only with this sympathetic understanding can people develop the kinds of openness to others which are required in a democratic society.

# Notes

1. Fuller comments can be found at https://gustavus.edu/english/whystudyliterature.php (Accessed 2 November 2017).
2. A full list of books that might be suitable for these purposes in a French classroom can be found at http://cache.media.eduscol.education.fr/file/Litterature/80/9/LISTE_DE_ReFeRENCE_CYCLE_3_2013_238809.pdf . Most of these have suggestions for lesson plans and exercises that can be found through an internet search.

# References

Armstrong, J. M. (1988). *The Unsaid Anna Karenina*. Basingstoke: Macmillan.
Ball, S. (2012), 'The Making of a Neoliberal Academic'. *Research in Secondary Education*, 2(1): 29–31.

Bromwich, D. (1996). 'Rat Poison'. *London Review*, 18(20): 13–15.

Council of Europe. (2015). *Teaching Controversial Issues Through Education for Democratic Citizenship and Human Rights*. (EDC/HRE) Training Pack for Teachers. Brussels, EU.

Davies, B. (2003). 'Death to Critique and Dissent? The Policies and Practices of New Managerialism and of "Evidence-Based Practice"'. *Gender and Education*, 15: 91–103.

Dewey, J. (1897). 'My Pedagogic Creed'. In Jo-Ann Boyson (Ed.), *The Collected Works of John Dewey, 1882–1953*, Early Works Vol. 5, 2nd Release e-edition. Carbondale and Edwardsville: Southern Illinois Press.

Dewey, J. (1909). 'Moral Principles in Education'. In Jo-Ann Boyson (Ed.), *The Collected Works of John Dewey, 1882–1953*, Middle Works Vol. 4, 2nd Release e-edition. Carbondale and Edwardsville: Southern Illinois Press.

Dewey, J. (1922). 'Human Nature and Conduct'. In Jo-Ann Boyson (Ed.), *The Collected Works of John Dewey, 1882–1953*, Middle Works Vol. 14, 2nd Release e-edition. Carbondale and Edwardsville: Southern Illinois Press.

Elliot, A. (1981). *Child Language*. Cambridge: Cambridge University Press.

Evans, M. (1988). *Reflecting on Anna Karenina*. London: Routledge.

Gleeson, D. and C. Husbands. (2004). *The Performing School*. London: Routledge.

Heldt, B. (1992). *Terrible Perfection*. Bloomington: Indiana University Press.

Isaac Mwita, J. (2000). 'Performance Management Model: A Systems-Based Approach to Public Service Quality'. *International Journal of Public Sector Management*, 13(1): 19–37.

Johnson, B. (1982). 'Teaching Ignorance: L'Ecole des Femmes'. *Yale French Studies*, 63: 165–82. Retrieved 11 March 2017 from http://www.jstor.org/stable/2929838.

Johnson, R. (2008). 'Federico García Lorca's Theater and Spanish Feminism'. *Anales De La Literatura Española Contemporánea*, 33(2): 251–81. Retrieved from http://www.jstor.org/stable/27742554.

Mandelker, A. (1993). *Framing Anna Karenina: Tolstoy, the Woman Question and the Victorian Novel*. Ohio: Ohio State University Press.

Marks, E. (1978). 'Women and Literature in France'. *Signs: Journal of Women in Culture and Society*, 3(4): 832–42.

Mead, G. (1934). *Mind, Self and Society*. Chicago, IL: University of Chicago Press.

McCall, G. (1977). 'The Social Looking-Glass: A Sociological Perspective on Self-Development'. In T. Mischel (Ed.), *The Self: Psychological and Philosophical Issues*, 274–91. Oxford: Basil Blackwell.

Moi, T. (2008). '"I Am Not a Woman Writer": About Women, Literature and Feminist Theory Today'. *Feminist Theory*, 9(30): 259–71.

Murray, J. (2012). 'Performativity Cultures and Their Effects on Teacher Educators' Work'. *Research in Teacher Education*, 2(2): 18–23.

Nussbaum, M. (1996a). *Education for Democratic Citizenship*. Lecture delivered on the occasion of the awarding of the degree of Doctor Honoris Causa at the Institute of Social Studies, The Hague, The Netherlands, 9 March.

Nussbaum, M. (1996b). 'Education and Democratic Citizenship: Capabilities and Quality Education'. *Journal of Human Development and Capabilities*, 7(3): 385–95.

Nussbaum, M. (1996c). *Poetic Justice: The Literary Imagination and Public Life*. Boston, MA: Beacon Press.

Nussbaum, M. (2010). *Not for Profit: Why Democracy Needs the Humanities*. Princeton, NJ: Princeton University Press.

Oakeshott, M. (1972). 'Education: The Engagement and Its Frustration'. In T. Fuller (Ed.), *The Voice of Liberal Learning*. New Haven, CT; London: Yale University Press.

Pring, R. (2012). *The Life and Death of Secondary Education for All*. London; New York: Routledge.

Quarantelli, E., and J. Cooper. (1966). 'Self-Conceptions and Others: A Further Test of Meadian Hypotheses'. *Sociological Quarterly*, 7: 281–97.

Ravitch, D. (2013). *Reign of Error: The Hoax of the Privatization Movement and the Danger to America's Public Schools*. New York: Alfred A. Knopf.

Small, H. (2013). 'The Literary Example in Moral Philosophy Today'. *Boundary*, 40(2): 41–51.

Tebben, M. (1999). 'Speaking of Women: Molière and Conversation at the Court of Louis XIV'. *Modern Language Studies*, 29(2): 189–207. Retrieved from http://www.jstor.org/stable/3195414.

Warner, M. (2003). 'To Be a Man'. *Guardian Books*. Retrieved Saturday 26 April 2003 23.35 BST from https://www.theguardian.com/books/2003/apr/26/classics.albertcamus.

# 2

# Literature in Primary Languages Classrooms

*Jane Jones*

## Introduction

In this chapter, I highlight possibilities for putting literature at the centre of primary languages teaching and learning. Children enjoy their language learning, and opportunities to engage with literature can readily enhance this experience where enjoyment is at a premium in the overcrowded and pressurized primary curriculum. The general benefits of early language learning have been extensively documented, and the contribution of literature to children's emotional, cultural and linguistic literacy, reading skills and to their overall development according to, for example, Day and Bamford (1998) and Ellis and Brewster (2014) is considerable. However, a note of caution is timely for children's opportunities in these respects are far from equal as much depends on the nature of languages provision in a school's curriculum as well as the availability of books at home.

I use a comparative lens to look into primary classrooms in Germany and Spain as well as in English classrooms, seeking an insight into how teachers in different contexts use literature in their language teaching. My aim is to provide a kaleidoscope of practices and views about using literature to consider what we can learn from each other. Nodelman (2008) asserts that while children's literature is often selected by teachers and other adults, today's children have a greater opportunity to express their likes and preferences and to choose the books they want to read. It is for this reason that alongside the teachers' own accounts, I have asked about children's preferences.

Hans-Eberhard Piepho (2007) undertook extensive research with young language learners in Germany based on the use of narrative, a concept I use as an analytical tool. Piepho asserts that the most effective pedagogy throughout all the stages and ages of language learning centres on the use and generative potential of the narrative format in the form of books, stories (see Brandford, Chapter 4), poems and rhymes, to structure lessons to promote children's language learning growth.

# The context of the research: spaces for literature in the languages curriculum

Literature appears scarce at the secondary stage, with few opportunities for students to engage with literature per se. Some teachers mentioned Prévert's poems and sections of Le Petit Nicolas as well as commercially produced language magazines and Disney-type films in different languages. Maureen, a secondary head of MFL, works texts in to her scheme of work and finds her Year 9 pupils, for example, are greatly motivated by chunks of text, accompanied by the audiobook, from *Mala Suerte* by Gonzalez and Orejudo about a very clumsy, forgetful woman called Africa. Maureen commented, 'With pre-reading and follow-up tasks, it fits nicely into a module in which students describe themselves and other people'.

Although older learners, ironically, may have the language competence that enables them to cross the threshold into the sphere of personal engagement with real literature, it is a stage of learning that, sadly, the majority of learners at present are unlikely to reach. As is so often the case, the constraints of the curriculum and pressures seemingly militate against reading literature.

It is usually not until students move into post-16 language learning that they have the opportunity to engage with 'real literature'. It is an enjoyable and formative experience, and most people will remember the 'set texts' they studied at post-16 for a variety of reasons.

## Reflection point

Think back to your early reading of literature at some point in your education in a foreign language. Choose a text. How and why do you remember this text? What emotions does this memory give rise to? What lasting impact did it have on you?

Literature is defined in the OED as 'writing of some merit'. This seems to invoke for many notions of the classical canon of literature and, as a result, teachers often cannot conceive of such literature in the MFL curriculum before the post-16 phrase. However, the ALL Literature wiki curated by Steven Fawkes, author of Chapter 8 in this volume, shows the comprehensive interpretation of what literature means to language teachers. The inclusive list has all types of texts, both informative, for example, brochures, and imaginative texts such as stories and narratives and with which teachers can more readily identify. I work with this broad and common-sense definition of literature and use the above terms interchangeably.

The KS2 Languages National Curriculum (DfE, 2013: 2) places importance on pupils being able 'to explore the patterns and sounds of language through songs and rhymes … discover and develop an appreciation of a range of writing in the language studied … appreciate stories, songs, poems and rhymes in the language'. In the light of this, primary school children seemingly fare rather better than their secondary peers for even where learning time is restricted and the focus tends to be on vocabulary and short sentence–level teaching, many primary teachers manage to make use of story, rhyme and poems in both written form and through oral recounting.

# What do teachers in different contexts do with literature in their primary languages classroom?

As a comparative linguist, I was keen to explore the place of literature in the various languages classrooms in different contexts. To this end, I spent time with primary teachers in Germany and Spain as well as in England. I present the teachers' own accounts for readers to reflect on. I looked at children's books in libraries and bookshops in the three countries. I found classics, modern texts and a cross-cultural literature in which 'caterpillars' and 'gruffalos' and the like abound. Teachers will, of course, need to sort the literary wheat from the chaff in making sound evaluative judgement to establish intrinsic and pedagogic 'merit'.

## Window of research

Spend some time exploring children's literature in different languages. What would your personal criteria be for work 'of merit'? How would you evaluate the pedagogic value of some of the books you have looked at?

Start with the work of Ellis and Brewster (2014: 19) and comment, for example, on their criteria of literary devices, content, illustrations, educational potential and values *inter alia*. Now do an internet search on 'criteria for selecting children's literature'. Put together a list of common criteria and note any significant differences. How do you interpret these criteria, what criteria are important for you with literature in other languages and what would you add? On the basis of your chosen criteria, apply these to three books/texts, theorize and justify your analysis in terms of 'merit' and pedagogic value.

Let us now open a few classroom doors and observe colleagues from different schools in different countries teaching their languages.

# A primary school in North Rhine-Westphalia, Germany

Farina, a recently qualified primary school teacher, first mentioned the wide gap in reading scores and opportunities between those children where the home backgrounds support their children's reading and those where children have minimal support. She then described how she uses books in her language lessons:

> Mostly the little ones read German storybooks that show lots of pictures often with pictures of words they cannot read yet. The older ones read storybooks concerning their interests. Sometimes the class reads the same book together. Either the teacher or the children decide on the choice of book.
>
> We also use story books for particular social learning purposes. If the class has trouble with bullying, the school choses books that deal with that topic. Same with the topic of multicultural learning. The book 'Who's in the loo?' is very popular, a story about children who want to go to the toilet at the zoo but an octopus is blocking it. In fact the octopus is teaching the children to wash their hands so it is a story but also about hygiene.
>
> Often pupils get to see the cover first, before they start reading the book. They start talking about it and might think about the content. Some teachers even hide the title of the book, so the children can focus on the picture. Either the teacher starts reading out the book or the children do it one after the other. Most of the time they read until a chapter ends. Then the children get a task to work on what they have read. Often it starts with summarizing the content. The children and the teacher often talk about characters and feelings and think about what might happen next. Sometimes children write their own chapter or find another end to the story. We implement a reading diary where pupils have to write important facts about what they just have read, their own feelings about a part they have read or feelings about a character from the book.
>
> Mostly the children have to read a few pages / or read at least 20 minutes at home. Sometimes writing texts, for example writing in their reading diaries, needs to be done at home as well.
>
> Many books that we use in the primary English lessons are authentic picture books.
>
> The children do not read books by themselves. Usually the teacher does a storytelling lesson. Books we use a lot are The Very Hungry Caterpillar, The Gruffalo, Snore, Monkey Puzzle, Peppa Pig and The Mr Men which we have in both German and English. We typically work with picture cards for the book – the text of the book is broken down into flashcards – or any other additional material. Activities can be a role play, a worksheet with true/false sentences or anything else that fits the content of the book.
>
> I usually start by introducing new vocabularies before they start reading the book to make sure that the children are able to understand key words. Then I read out the book one/two/three times depending on the English level of the pupils so they get a feeling for how it sounds. I often try to activate this by making noises (for example while reading the book 'Snore'). After reading the book there are many activities like the memory game (with pictures and vocabularies), finding the right order of pictures cards of the story or writing short texts. I might occasionally ask them to practise some words at home.

The Nordrhein-Westfalen Ministry of Education website positions reading and access to a full range of texts in both German and in English as central to children's overall development. Farina illustrates Piepho's point about how teachers need to set the stage to create an atmosphere that invites the children to explore issues beyond the text. She shows how engagement with literature evolves from picture books, creating the internal images that allow children to move to more complex stories.

**Children's comments**

Soraya, 6: Ich mag 'Der König der Löwen'. Das Buch ist witzig, besonders Rafiki ist lustig. Ich mag das Buch auch, weil Simba da geboren wird und weil es das Buch als Film gibt. Die Geschichte ist spannend und schön.

(I like 'the lion king'. It is a funny book, especially Rafiki is funny. I also like the book, because Simba was born and there is a movie of the book. The story is exciting and a nice story.)

Sven, 8: Das Buch 'Der Grüffelo' ist mein Lieblingsbuch, weil man am Anfang gar nicht weiß, wer der Grüffelo ist. Die Maus ist so klein, aber sehr schlau und macht den anderen Tieren Angst. Der Grüffelo sieht witzig aus und das Ende der Geschichte ist cool.

(My favourite book is 'The Gruffalo', because while reading the book you do not know who the Gruffalo really is. The mouse is so small, but very smart and frightens the other animals. The Gruffalo looks funny and the end of the story is very cool.)

# A primary school in Madrid

Following a decision by the Community of Madrid in 2006 to provide Content and Language Integrated Learning (CLIL)-type teaching in English in certain subjects – Science and Natural Science, with optional Arts and Crafts, PE and Music – in Spanish primary schools in Madrid, children have the opportunity to read many types of text in English in school, both fiction and non-fiction. This is not without its challenges for the less secure teachers and learners. Ana, an experienced teacher, told me what the children read in language lessons:

Four year old children can usually recite popular Spanish poems and riddles and five year old learners have their individual reading books. Tales are very important because of content, structure and vocabulary. We do projects about the readings, role-plays, telling stories to practise oral expression, learning poems, songs and rhymes by heart, reading in silence/out loud, doing comprehension activities, playing games related to the stories, relating the readings to different areas: drawing, calculating, talking about history, about time … and we often watch a video of the book if there is one at the end.

In a recent lesson, my aims were to engage the students in reading and specifically to improve vocabulary: synonyms and antonyms. We looked at the pictures trying to predict what is going to happen. We talked about different situations (problems) related to the text giving personal opinions about what they would do in those situations. We did some shared reading in groups of 4. Once everyone had finished there was time for discussing a little if they liked it or not. We listened to the story using the digital board. To finish, we played a game in which I read the story to the class, changing some key words for antonyms or synonyms. As the students realized one word was not the right one they changed it. They really like this activity.

Normally it is quite easy to make young learners feel engaged with reading. In my opinion the big problem is that they do not read that much at home and as they grow up they feel demotivated as the 'only' thing they read are the books their teachers reads to them. The children are always asked to read the story to their favourite teddy at home and bring some pictures of the story. I motivate them to do things at home giving some ideas and as they feel proud when they come to class and show their peers what they've done.

In their English lessons, there is more storytelling. It can be supported with flashcards, realia (if possible) and body language. Tales with pop-ups and many visuals are also used, such as 'The Very Hungry Caterpillar' and 'The Colour Monster'. Older ones usually read the stories included in their text books. Most of them are comic strips that appear at the beginning of each unit and are related to the topic object of study. Songs, rhymes and tongue twisters are also very common. They then progress to a graded reader per term. Activities include putting in order the events of the stories, inventing different endings and discussing in class. We also do word search or crossword activities. We act out or use TPR activities to check understanding and introduce more vocabulary. In the following lesson, my aims were to learn more vocabulary about the sea, to be able to use adjectives related to colour and size in order to describe animals and to learn to value the importance of respect and friendship. The story is 'Swimmy the Fish'.

I presented different kinds of fish with flashcards. The students listened and repeated their names. We played a game with the flashcards. I introduced the story and the students predicted what was going to happen. Then, they listened to the story as they read it. In groups of 4 they had to answer some comprehension questions, using words related to colour, shape and size in order to describe the animals. Each group had a vocabulary bank with terms they might find useful but might not have memorised yet. Then, there was one activity with different pieces of paper which they had to put in order to make the story. Finally, there was a puzzle with an image from the story to play with (see Figure 2.1). We then acted out the story.

**Figure 2.1** Children completing fish puzzle.

**Figure 2.2** Children's story display board.

As a second example, recently we were reading stories about the circus (both in English and Spanish). The children made a big poster (see Figure 2.2) that they prepared in groups in collaboration with older students from 5th and 6th Grade (they just live for that kind of activity). They also made clown costumes with their parents' help as they were invited to come into school to do this. It was a complete mess, but they enjoyed it so much. To finish, we went on a parade, as part of a whole school project which we uploaded on Youtube.

Ana evidences Piepho's claim that literature is a most effective tool for language learning, more so as a 'bottom-up' experience which engages the young learners in reading and listening comprehension, role plays, group work, individual decoding and personal interpretation. He also stresses the importance of teachers as communicators of stories, someone who enjoy telling stories and who hone their skills of presenting as Ana does.

**Children's comments**

Nico, 7: Me gustan mucho los libros de los dinosaurios porque tienen dientes, tienen fósiles, son muy antiguos … Y me gustan mucho los de los insectos porque los puedes tener de mascota, puedes ser famoso por eso. Y los de la naturaleza porque hay plantas muy venenosas y muy guays. Me gusta nuestro libro de Ciencias en inglés. Tiene un hámster que nos enseña las cosas que aprendemos.

(I like books about dinosaurs very much because they have teeth, fossils and are very ancient ... And I like the ones about insects a lot because you can have them as pets, you can become famous because of that. And the ones about nature because there are very poisonous plants and they are very cool. I like our Science book in English. It has a hamster who shows us things that we learn about.)

Juan, 7: Me gustan los libros de Geronimo Stilton porque son de aventuras y de amistades.

(I like books by Geronimo Stilton because they are about adventure and friendship.)

# A primary school in Almería, Spain

Isa's children enjoy many classics in their Spanish and English lessons:

Caperucita Roja, for example, Blancanieves y los Siete Enanitos, Aladín. They love a collection called 'Futbolísimo'. The older pupils usually read 'El Conde Lucanor', 'Las Fábulas de Esopo', 'Diario de Greg', the collection of Geronimo Stilton. The students always have one book in Spanish and one in English. They have a 'carnet de lector' and they must write when they started it, when they finished it, if they liked it or not and why. They must write if they would recommend it to anyone, would change the ending and sometimes write a book review

In one English lesson with grade 5, the topics were around: who we are, cultures, folktales, differences, present simple. I asked the students what they thought a folktale was as my lead in to a traditional Cinderella. Our first activity was popcorn reading where students read a sentence or two each, at the end of their section they say 'popcorn' (and name of classmate) and that person reads on, until they popcorn someone and so on until the end of the text and until everyone in the class has read at least once

We then looked at Ye Shen, Chinese Cinderella https://www.youtube.com/watch?v=WTsCk5fJYpo

This lead to class discussion about Impressions of the two tales, which one they like more and why, and asking the class to list (cultural) differences between the Chinese version and the classic one that we write on the board. The students then put these differences into a Venn diagram with a partner – at least 5 items in each part – and look for the similarities. Then finally we discuss the points and put into one big Venn on the board like this:

-Cinderella – lived in a house, had two step-sisters, fairy godmother grants her the wish, invited to a ball, dances/meets the prince, hurries home before midnight, glass slipper

-Both – were orphans, treated badly at home, forbidden to go to the ball/festival by their step-mother, both end up going because of a magical wish, very beautiful, lose a slipper, are found and happily married because of the slipper

-Ye Shen – lived in a cave, had only one step-sister, Gold Eyes is her only friend and his bones grant her the wish, invited to a festival, does not meet king at the festival, hurries home because she is afraid stepmother might recognize her, silk slipper, was mistaken for a thief

I then turned this into a language practice activity where the children had to create 4 comparison statements using the present simple tense e.g. Cinderella lives in a house, while Ye Shen lives in a cave, using the info from the Venn diagrams, and to finish for HW. The children really enjoy the books used in their English lessons.

According to Piepho, every narrative inherently contains nearly all linguistic phenomena, even at beginners' level, that the teacher can extract for her purposes. The Spanish teachers make use of this, Ana with her antonyms, Isa with her present simple focus. They are in not only working with books that the children enjoy but also meeting Cameron's (2001: 159) assertion for teachers to 'make the content accessible … and construct activities that offer language learning opportunities'.

---

**Children's comments**

Manu, 10: Me encantan las clases de inglés porque aprendo y me divierto a la vez. Me gustan mucho Nanny McPhee y the big bang porque es muy divertido y aprendo muchas cosas sobre el trabajo en equipo.

(I love English lessons because I learn and have fun at the same time. I like a lot Nanny McPhee and the big bang because it is fun and I learn a lot of things about teamwork.)

Rosa, 7: The Gingerbread Man me ha gustado mucho porque era de una galleta que se salía del horno, que la estaban cocinando y querían ir por ella porque olía súperbien. Fue muy emocionante.

(I really liked the GM because it was about a biscuit that left the oven where it was being cooked and they wanted to go after it because it smelt really good. It was very exciting.)

---

## Reflective point

What would you say are the similarities and differences of approach in the way that the teachers in Germany and Spain teach literature in their language lessons, and how would you account for these? What, for example, are the cultural frames, the educational values and the political influences?

# English primary schools

Reading and literacy in general are a lynchpin in the English National curriculum. It is useful for language teachers to know what literature the children we teach in primary languages are reading generally to provide a backdrop to compare what the children are doing in their MFL lessons.

## Suggested task

Arrange to observe English lessons/literacy work in some different primary schools. What are the children reading and enjoying? How do teachers work with intensive whole-class reading of texts? What opportunities are there for pupils to read for pleasure and what do they like? How could these experiences be related to the reading of texts in primary language lessons? Make notes on these items and construct a grid to show what explicit links could be made to support children's reading of literature in different languages.

# A primary school in Kent

The children in this pre-prep and prep school with children aged 2½ to 12 have a rich provision for literature in their language learning across both KS1 and KS2, in this case being Spanish. The teacher, Anaverde, includes many texts in her regular teaching:

> Normally the books are chosen to support the specific topics in terms of vocabulary, structure of the sentences etc. although sometimes we read for pleasure, to expose the children to Spanish texts. In some cases we read the books to see how much the vocabulary they can identify when read in context as a plenary at the end of a lesson or sometimes as a starter at the beginning. Sometimes the books are used to introduce new vocabulary such as the days of week using La pequeña oruga glotona or A qué sabe la luna to introduce wild animals and they constitute an important part of the lesson. This is a typical reading syllabus that I created:

---

*Year 2*
   *La pequeña oruga glotona* by Eric Carle (for days of the week and birthday party food)
   *Oso pardo, oso pardo* by Bill Martin, Jr, and Eric Carle (colours and farm animals)
   *Pinta ratones* by Ellen Stoll Walsh (colours)

*Year 3*
   Online story from http://cvc.cervantes.es: el colegio abandonado (school)
   *A qué sabe la luna* by Michael Grejniec (wild animals)
   *Hormiguita negra*, book of poems by Ana M. Romero Yebra (wild animals)

*Year 4*
   *A los marcianos les encantan los calzoncillos* by Claire Freedman and Ben Cort (clothes and the clothes shop)
   *La plaza*, poem by Antonio Machado (describing my city)
   *La sorpresa de Handa* by Eileen Browne (healthy eating and describing fruits)

*Year 5*
   *Monstruo triste, monstruo feliz* by Ed Emberly and Anne Miranda (personal character and feelings)
   *Mi ciudad* by Rebecca Treays (the town)

*Year 6*
   *El Grúfalo* by Julia Donaldson and Axel Sheffler (at the doctors', parts of the body, expressing pain)
   *Un elefante va a la ciudad* by Amit Grag (use of the simple past)

---

The aim with a recent year 2 infants' lesson was to learn the names of some farm animals, introduced through the book: Oso pardo, oso pardo, ¿qué ves ahí?. First I read the book slowly a couple of times. Children start joining in with the reading. As children are very familiar with this story they normally learn it in Spanish very quickly, with some children even learning it by heart. We also revise the colours. In order to visualize and try to remember the names of the animals we play a variation of the game heads down, thumbs up: children are shown cards with the pictures of the animals from the book and if they can remember the name they can stand up at the front of the class holding their card. Nine children stand at the front holding a card (one per animal on the book). They say/read their animal to the class. Then the rest of the class put their heads down and their thumbs up and the children with the card go around the classroom and pick one child each. Then, they return to the front of the class. The children that have been picked can then stand up and they have to guess who picked their thumb although they are only allowed to say the colour on the card, not the name of the child, for example: Teacher: ¿Quién fue? Child: El pato amarillo. If they guess, they swap places.

For the writing session, children are given printed cards with each animal. They have to write/copy one sentence on the card and then colour the picture of their animals. Children can make more than one. As they finish, the cards are collected and glued into a class book. Early finishers can colour the front cover of the book and copy the title. For the plenary I ask volunteer children to read one page of the new book. By the end, children have learnt the names of some animals, revised the colours and produced a class book.

With my year 6, I wanted to revise parts of the body. Before we start the topic 'At the doctors', children revise the parts of the body. Using a flipchart, children are presented with a Bart Simpson body and help me label as many parts of the body as they can remember. Once children have shown that they can remember the parts of the body, they are presented with a description of the Grúfalo. They don't know that this is the book. We go through the description together and then in pairs with the help of a dictionary they try to find the meaning of the words that they don't know and hopefully guess the character.

For the writing session, children use the new vocabulary they have learnt in the descriptive paragraph of the Grúfalo to create in pairs their own monster or creature. When they finish, they draw a picture. Some are used for display. At the end of the lesson, children read aloud and share their descriptions and pictures with the rest of the class. Children have revised the parts of the body, learnt new adjectives and features to make their descriptions more exciting, read and listened to Spanish descriptions of body parts in the wider context of a story.

There are lots of audio visual materials including stories such as from
http://www.lcfclubs.com/babelzoneNEW/
https://cvc.cervantes.es/ensenanza/mimundo/mimundo/default.html
Videos support children with special needs who have the same opportunities and join in as much as possible with the support of the LSA. Some children work with flash cards of the stories or picture books. All the children love the videos.

Anaverde's work with very young children reflects Nodelman's (1990: viii) assertion that 'illustrations-images … explain or clarify words'. Rosen (2017) writes that children bring the story they hear and the story they see in pictures together to make sense of it. In other words, children 'read' pictures that mediate meaning and the language before they are fully able to read and according to Piepho (2007: 7), they learn to create images for the new sound in their heads. He also suggests a reading list (as Anaverde has done) as 'each story is the foundation of understanding other stories' (2007: 24).

---

**Children's comments**

Darcy, 7: Oso pardo, oso pardo: 'because it was easy to understand with the pictures'.

Lexie, 9: ¡Mecachis, quiero ser grande! by Ricardo Alcantara and Emilio Urberuaga: 'it was kind of easy but I still used Google translator. It was really funny. I got it from the library and read it at home'.

Roberto, 8: A los marcianos les encantan los calzoncillos by Claire Freedman and Ben Cort: 'because it was very funny'.

---

# A primary school in South West London

Amy teaches in a mixed state primary school that has a bilingual arrangement to teach some of its subjects in French:

> We follow the national curriculum through reading lots of stories, acting them out when possible and children learn to perform a short French poem in year 4. We teach stories and poems in French e.g. la promenade de Monsieur Gentil. These can be used to pick up on particular grammatical features if a teacher wishes.
>
> We use literature extensively in our language lessons. At KS1, there are lots of stories, often French children's book or a well- known English book translated into French e.g. La Chenille qui fait des Trous. The children have French packs (book & CD recording of the book) which they take home each week from school and listen to. French stories are read to the children twice a week. The texts get progressively harder/longer from year 3 to year 6. Here, French stories are read to the children twice a week by a native speaker (usually a teaching assistant).
>
> We also do 'Guided Reading' where groups of up to 6 children read a book in French with a teacher for 20 mins. Children read aloud in French, learn vocabulary and pronunciation and answer questions about the text in French. The focus is the book itself, with focus on French pronunciation and general comprehension. Texts are usually French children's books as mentioned. We have about 20 books for the children to read over the year starting with Folio Cadet – premières lectures e.g. translations of Tony Ross's books.
>
> From year 4 upwards, children read non-fiction books in Guided Reading as well in our French topic (CLIL) lessons. This will usually be a simplified version of an authentic text from a French website or French information books written for children. I would use the text in a similar way to how they use a story in English. I would read the text to the class, with some clarification of meaning throughout and then we would do an activity based on the text, for example in the book 'Un Lion à Paris', the children might discuss/write answers to the question 'pourquoi le lion a-t-il peur?' in French.

Here is a sample lesson plan, for C'est moi le plus beau' story- writing work (KQ are Key Questions)

To start, we sing Bonjour Salut ... Ça va? And go around the circle. I introduce the new question: Est-ce que tu as des frères ou des soeurs? I ask some children to share responses then we practise in pairs.

KQ: What are storywords/ time connectives? When and why might we use them in stories in English? Talk partners and feedback.

KQ: Pourquoi ils sont aussi utiles en français? Talk partners and feedback.

I give out storywords for children to match up (French and English) – 5 mins in partners. Go through and allow children to correct/ change their work.

KQ: Which ones were easier to work out? Discuss cognates . . .

KQ: Can you think of any strategies to remember the words? Give example of 'en suite' bathroom being **next to** and linked to a bedroom! Give children a chance to think of a couple in partners and feedback.

For the main part of the lesson, we re-read 'C'est Moi le Plus Beau' – children join in with '«Qui est le plus beau?» demande le loup.' whenever it comes up.

I stop at 'il rencontre alors un petit dragon' and write 'il rencontre alors ...' This is where our stories will begin. We recap key phrases from text (from last week's session):

'Qui est le plus beau?' demande le loup.

... répond le loup.

C'est moi le plus beau'.

Quel/Quelle . . .!

Bonjour . . .

Les petits ... (change 'lardons' to their own idea!)

Le loup croise/fait une promenade . . .

I explain that by adapting these, the children can mirror the sound of the original story.

Children for independent learning can carry on writing their endings with their partner, using the key phrases, French dictionaries, asking teacher. Sometimes for homework, children might have a short text in French and some comprehension questions. This is usually about an aspect of French culture we have learnt about in class and is taken from a French children's website such as 'Hellokids' that provides a wide range of reading of all kinds, stories, non-fiction, BD all in illustrated bite-sized texts and access to children's culture in another language.

Amy's approach supports Piepho's view that pupils can be stimulated to construct new texts based on their experience with the pattern of a story, to be able to write their own adaptations, endings, etc. Amy's lessons also show evidence of collaborative skills being developed with the reading exercises in guided reading groups, akin to 'group reading and writing conferences' advocated by Fitzgerald (1994: 33) as 'social communicative acts' and a way to develop criticality.

---

**Children's comments**

Dominique, 8: J'aime 'C'est moi le plus beau'. J'aime le loup. Il est beau!'

George, 10: J'aime l'histoire des pirates et 'Le Gruffalo' en français. Je lis aussi The Gruffalo en anglais.

# A primary school in the north of England

The children in this school have regular timetabled time for their language learning at KS1 and KS2. Furthermore the language is German, seemingly a popular choice. The teacher, Sue, talks about this and how she uses literature in her German lessons:

> The parents know they will take French in the secondary school so they are quite pleased that they do German. Parents sometimes come in to join in the lessons and I send German crib sheets home for the parents.
>
> I use lots of literature, loads of books and videos as the focal point of my lessons. The scheme of work for primary can easily be written around books. An absolute favourite of mine has always been Pippi Langstrumpf. She is a superhero, been around for generations and children today can relate easily to her life style. They see that her animal companions, a monkey and a horse are real friends and the way she dresses with odd stockings and super comfy if a little odd clothes perfect for just throwing on. She more or less does her own things but she goes to school, is respectful most of the time and kind. It's the perfect combo for children who would like to live in their imagination in the way she does. Her full name in German is Pippilotta Viktualia Rollgardina Schokominza Efraimstochter Langstrumpf that the children love. We sing the name and I hold a competition to see who can memorise it.
>
> There are loads of resources but an absolute favourite of mine is the video of Pippi going to school on a winter day. This is how typically I teach this lesson sequence with KS2 classes: https://www.youtube.com/watch?v=_Sz3qmApP5E
>
> Watch the video for about 10 minutes from where she gets up and has breakfast with her horse before going to school until when she comes back enjoying the snow and nature all around. There is limited language used, so the children can enjoy a viewing as a visual treat. Then I introduce key words with the next viewings- horse- monkey- clothes- stockings- breakfast- a bit of vocab practice then we construct sentences to tell the story. In fact they construct the story before they see the book version. Over a series of lessons, we learn sentences that I relate to some sentences in the book by heart, then the children act out the story making it their own with their own twiddles and some start writing their own. One group insisted the pupils who play the horse and monkey wore odd socks. They always but always bring in odd socks to wear in these lessons. It is obligatory to put your socks on to sing Pippi's song. There are lots of cross-curricular activities to do and Astrid Lindgren's website is a great source of inspiration.
>
> As well as some useful German that relates to the scheme of work- animals, clothes, seasons, at schools, there are big children's themes to relate to- living your dream world, being a bit different, whacky and unconventional, being resourceful, developing resilience, an awareness of kindness. We have lots of discussions about these things. Target language stuff is target language, but my lessons are more than that, they are about exploring childhood through different eyes.

With regard to Sue's teaching, Piepho's point that the children can develop strategies of understanding and means to tell stories of their own fantasy daily routines in the foreign language and become more independent is relevant. As Sue shows, the context is carefully set by using familiar words and the children hear the story repeatedly through various media to enable them to reconstruct and then construct their own version of a story.

**Children's comments**

Sophie, 9. Ich mag Pippi weil ein Pferd und einen Affen ihre Freunde sind.
   (I like Pippi because she has a horse friend and a monkey friend.)
   Hasan, 7. She can be 'home alone' and do what she wants.

## Window of research

You will have noted the similar book titles, childhood themes and storylines, lots of animals and quirky beings in the literature that has been cited. Why do you think this is so? What does the research say about these eternal and universal themes in children's literature? To what extent are they culturally sensitive?

Peter Hunt, for example, writes, 'Children's books have a long history around the world, and they have absorbed into themselves elements of folk, fairy tale and the oral tradition. It is also possible to perceive similar patterns through the world' (2005: 4).

Respond to these points by reading Cameron (2001), Nodelman (2008) and Hunt (2005) as well as anything else that interests you on the topic.

# What then can teachers learn from each other's classrooms?

In this section, I highlight key points of interest and learning from the teachers (all primary generalists) and their lessons with literature.

## A children's shared literature landscape

The lessons highlight a shared teacher understanding in terms of choice of book and theme, as to what children enjoy and can relate to. The pupils also share a similar and recognizable children's literature landscape and derive similar messages about life from this. Quentin Blake (2017) wrote that when children can see themselves in a book, then they can see themselves in the world. The experience of literature in another language gives children an opportunity to see other children in other spaces in other worlds as the children who feature in this chapter have shown. The children were able to make thoughtful cultural comparisons between the Cinderella versions in Isa's lesson, for example,

## A continuum of bilingual teaching

The bilingual nature of the approaches described, enacted to varying degrees, reflect Lo Bianco's (2013) view of a continuum of bilingual teaching approach. In Germany, there is considerable exposure to texts in English in daily English lessons where teachers can create moments of contingent bilingual teaching. In Madrid, because of the Commune bilingual programme, bilingual teaching is towards the strong CLIL end of the continuum, packaged within subjects. All primary languages teachers can locate a space on the bilingual continuum to match their particular context for ultimately, it is no more than normal age-appropriate teaching with, as one infant teacher in an English school put it, 'making as many of the activities and interactions bilingual'. She was teaching her three and four year olds to sing songs in both English and French and to 'read' picture books in both languages.

It was noticeable that the children in all the schools liked having books in two languages, including non-fiction. This affordance provides an important linguistic and accessible safety net for the learners, especially useful for children with special needs.

# Imaginative, creative and multisensory teaching and learning

The creativeness shown by the teachers to make full use of literature shows skill and imagination. Their practices reflect individual teacher cultures, personalities and preferences but have adaptable transfer value to other contexts. Teachers can take bits they like and make these their own. Curtain and Pesola (1994) wrote that language learning is most effective when experienced holistically, with hands-on activities and concrete experiences with the use of props, visuals and realia in an interdisciplinary and multisensory framework. In this, the primary languages teachers excel. Astrid Lindgren, creator of Pippi Longstocking, reflecting on reading as a child, 'looking at the strange black squiggles … something that engaged your entire being – sight, smell, touch – more intensely than anything else in a child's world' (AstridLindgren.com), resonates with the attention paid by the teachers to the development of the whole child with literature.

# All the four skills and grammar!

The teachers have worked with all four skills, as and when appropriate (Doyé & King, 2012), with no dogmatic avoidance of the written word. Indeed, Fitzgerald (1994: 33) advocates some sort of reading and writing as soon as possible, 'always adapted to the learner's level in the new language'. The narrative structure that according to Piepho drives the learning has been fully used to underpin whole language growth, exploiting known conventions of literature such as repetition, building new language on previous knowledge, thus providing a basis for ever more complex stories. The teachers artfully use the books to develop both lexical content and grammatical sensitivity. The teachers are very explicit about this Anaverde's Spanish grammatically annotated reading list and Ana's clearly defined lesson aims. This enables the children to construct their own literature, in both oral and written forms.

# Collaboration and independence

There is evidence of considerable collaborative activity as well as independent learning with literature in languages in these lessons, a powerful 'tight-loose' learning yolk. The former features in all of the lessons with whole class activity and group tasks, projects, film-making, parades and group reading and writing, all in authentic, collaborative, sociocultural active learning contexts. As far as independent learning goes, all the teachers suggested some home learning or practice and the 'books to go home' practice in two languages serves to promote independent bilingual learning, giving children real choices to enjoy literature in their own time and for their own purposes. The key to this would be Piepho's argument for a class library as the best way to stimulate children to read according to their own abilities, the point at which a child starts reading a book entirely in the foreign language differing from child to child.

# A role for literature in primary to secondary transition

The use of literature as described indicates an opportunity largely missed but one that could be a key point of focus for transitional learning given the familiarity the children coming into secondary school have with story and picture books. Indeed, many primary teachers are creating a template for perfect transitional learning tasks that embody listening and reading skills and simple storytelling and writing. The 'book per topic' approach advocated by Anaverdi would slot nicely into the 'topic-based with grammar' learning that is prominent in secondary schools as Maureen demonstrated at the beginning of the chapter. The older pupils in Amy's school continue their reading groups with exponentially more complex readers providing continuing reading skills development. Rather than reject 'literature' on the grounds of lack of time, well-chosen readers and story/poetry websites as well as short extracts and song lyrics can provide a transitional focus as well as a longer-term fully embeddable resource for teachers to use to develop all four skills, grammar in context and cultural learning.

# Conclusion

In conclusion, the teachers in this chapter have positioned using literature as central and not peripheral to their pedagogy of primary languages teaching and learning. The children have been shown to be very active not just with objects and skills learning but also in constructing their own meaning from literature and creating their own narratives using a range of strategies that they have developed exponentially. Above all, the children come to see the mirror image of language for real in literature in a way that is meaningful for them and that enables them to develop and enjoy a personal emotional response to what they hear, see and read, the 'interpreting response' that encourages 'leaps of interpretation' as expounded by Rosen (2017). Restricting young learners to lessons comprising decontextualized vocabulary is an impoverished experience at the side of such rich and personalized linguistic, literary and joyful experiences that have been described. As Piepho writes (2007: 7), 'Sie sind keine Zuckerchen im Alltabrei des harten Unterrichtsgeschehens, sondern vielmehr der Kern des Sprachwachstumsprozesses': narratives, he says, using a metaphor of daily grind/porridge, are not just bits of sugar to sweeten the daily grind of teaching ('brei' on its own means 'porridge'; see below]) but they are at the heart of the language growth process.

Primary languages teaching would benefit from a reframing with literature at the centre for the 'full porridge mix experience' (albeit with time and resourcing). However, the 'porridge approach' needs to take heed of Piepho's assertion that the use of narrative needs to be a well-planned process. Cameron (2001: 160) is also concerned that teachers avoid 'fuzzy thinking about how children learn' and 'aim to think clearly about how tasks are organised and what children should learn from them'. The comparison of classroom practices has shown both teachers and children in different contexts engaging purposefully and strategically with literature in spaces that are inextricably intertwined through cultural links, pedagogic practices and what turns out to be a shared literature.

As part of their personalized professional development, teachers could valuably visit others' classrooms in other contexts. This would enable them to see how literature is anchored into language lessons and enhances children's lives as well as gain inspiration for new ideas. It may be that the primary languages teacher provides a literature experience that some children might otherwise never have as the German teacher, Farina, mentioned. As such, literature attains a critical role in children's language learning and general literacy, a challenge well within the grasp of the extraordinarily resourceful community of primary languages teachers.

# References

Blake, Q. (2017). 'Drawing Is the Most Important Thing There Is'. *Telegraph Magazine*. Accessed 12 August 2018 from https://www.telegraph.co.uk/books/authors/drawing-important-thing-quention-blake- talks-lauren-child/.

Cameron, L. (2001). *Teaching Languages to Young Learners*. Cambridge: Cambridge University Press.

Curtain, H. and C. A. Pesola. (1994). *Languages and Children. Making the Match*. New York: Longman

Day, R. and J. Bamford. (1998). *Extensive Reading in the Second Language Classroom*. Cambridge: Cambridge University Press.

DfE. (2013). *National Curriculum Languages Programme of Study for KS2*. London: GOV. UK.

Doyé, P. and B. King. (2012). *Kindergarten Goes Bilingual. Englisch im bilingualen Kindergarten*. Hildesheim: Georg Olms Verlag.

Ellis, G. and J. Brewster. (2014). *Tell It Again! The Storytelling Handbook for Primary English Language Teachers*. London: The British Council.

Fitzgerald, J. (1994). 'How Literacy Emerges: Foreign Language Implications'. *Language Learning Journal*, 9: 32–5.

Hunt, P. (2005). (Ed.) *Key Essays from the 2nd Edition of the International Companion Encyclopedia of Children's Literature*. London: Routledge.

Lindgren, A. 'Section: Life: Reading'. Accessed December 2017 from www.AstridLindgren.com.

Lo Bianco, J. (2013). 'CLIL in Australia: The Importance of Context'. *International Journal of Bilingual Education and Bilingualism*, 16(4): 395–410.

Nodelman, P. (1990). *Words about Pictures. The Narrative Art of Children's Picture Books.* Athens: University of Georgia Press.

Nodelman, P. (2008). *The Hidden Adult: Defining Children's Literature.* Baltimore, MD: John Hopkins University Press.

Piepho, H.-E. (2007). *Narrative Dimensionen im Fremdsprachenunterricht.* Herausgegeben Börner, von and Edelhoff, C. Braunschweig: Schroedel, Diesterweg, Klinkhardt.

Rosen, M. (2017). 'Some Thoughts on Why Picture Books are So Important'. *michaelrosenblog.blogspot.co.uk*. Blog of 28 November 2017. Accessed December 2017.

# 3

# Literature and Drama for Transfer

## *Jennifer Eddy*

## Introduction

This chapter provides a framework for performance assessment task design using literature as works of art for creating an integrated, aesthetic experience for the learner. The model encourages creativity and critical thinking skills as learners use dramatic exploration to transform one work of art into another. To what extent can creativity, drama and novelty play a role in task design for understanding literature? What does transfer look like for the learner? When the learners achieve transfer, they can use knowledge and skills differently than how they were originally acquired to create something new. Learners will understand that literature can inspire other aesthetic genres. Artists, composers and authors do this all the time; our students can too.

First, we examine the role of literature as authentic material for creative intercultural competence and transfer tasks in the curriculum. How aesthetic education, creativity and drama are informed by pedagogical theory and world language education practice are critical questions during the chapter. Second, we will explore dramatic exploration through integrated task design with the three modes of communication, interpretive, interpersonal and presentational, an assessment system in world language education. Finally, we will see how these unfold into transfer tasks for personal and current engagement with the piece. This helps learners see that literature is not fixed or static and that they also can create something new. These tasks encourage flexibility, tolerance of ambiguity and autonomy, all key characteristics of intercultural competence. They move the learner beyond inert, rote facts that maintain detachment toward engaged connection, innovation and transfer. By transforming these works of art, these novel tasks effectively shorten the creative and cultural distance between the author and learner.

## How does the learner engage personally and respond creatively to literature through drama?

Language is creativity by design. An artist always moves beyond what is given to reveal a new vision, message or question; that act of creativity engages us to respond and react to it. So it is with language, in that in every act of communication, there is our creative element responding to the unexpected. With the focus of language programs on flexible, communicative practice for proficiency, literature is often viewed as a fixed and static artefact, detached from the present experience of day-to-day communication. Literature is still taught often in isolation, housed in a curricular cloister on its own, relegated to upper levels in the curriculum which unfortunately many students might not attain. The learner who does not engage with literature as a work of art misses out on creative response and the possibility of new interpretations.

Creative, novel response is the hallmark of drama and transfer. Transfer is defined as using knowledge and skills differently than originally presented or taught, within a new situation, context, problem or product with few cues or supports (McTighe & Wiggins, 2005; Eddy, 2007, 2014, 2017). These transfer tasks are not drills on isolated skill components but instead are authentic, formative participatory tasks that use a repertoire flexibly to solve problems or create novel products of value. The tasks look at assessment differently and more qualitatively than would a quiz. Transfer tasks show both student and teacher the distinction between mechanized drill practice and creative performance. They train the learner in adaptability and adjustment, putting to rest predictable practice which cannot prepare learners for authentic language use. Swaffar and Arens (2005) define language itself as 'a set of culture-based performances, situated in various public, private, and disciplinary contexts' (20). Applied to language learning, transfer tasks become the dramatic and participatory vignettes, the culture-based performances of a larger curricular story. Drama enables transfer by creating a more porous boundary from oft-rigid classroom spaces (Singh, 2004).

## Performance assessment tasks for transfer

Change the genre. Turn a dance into a song or poem, a song into a play or film, a painting into a poem, novel, play, short story, etc.

    Write the curator notes for a museum piece

    Compose an Ode to a simple object or to an idea in the piece

    Create a story about the work from a child's view

    Design a museum exhibit

    Write a movie or theatrical plot based on a song, painting, literary work or photograph

    Create own music video from the original work

With transfer tasks, the learner demonstrates understanding of a concept by demonstrating it within the context of something else. When learners solve a novel problem or create a product of value beyond classroom walls, they extend themselves and their understanding of the work in yet another way. These integrated and participatory tasks ask learners to reach into the literary piece and react to individual, communal recursive life themes and issues, allowing them to respond with novelty. When this happens, learners do not experience the literature as static, transient, foreign or local; instead, their solutions enable personal and present connectedness and acquaintance.

## Reflection question

Consider different literary texts, styles and genres in your classroom. Are there ones that lend themselves better to dramatic performance tasks for transfer?

Literature is considered culturally authentic material, made by and for the speakers of that language and not pedagogically prepared for classroom use (Galloway, 1998). Through its many genres, literature tells a culture's story, unfolded over time and reaching across it. It presents the range of social backgrounds with which to explore and empathize (Collie & Slater, 1996; Cunico, 2005; Koritz, 2005). It provides enduring ideas on human issues, intercultural perspectives, practices, beliefs, patterns, contexts and concerns that deeply matter. It offers human experiences, desires, public and private behaviours and lessons learned or not. These all beckon us to connect personally in order to solve life's questions and problems that oft transcend temporal and cultural boundaries toward intercultural competence.

Because novels, short stories, poems and plays are not pedagogically prepared, the material is not arranged cleanly (Nance, 2010) with the predictability of teacher-developed scripts. So much of K-12 teacher training is steeped in routine and predictable patterns, traditional language teaching methodology even more so. This prepares the teacher and subsequently the learner to expect mechanized practice with content pedagogy, the complete antithesis of real-world expectations for creative and flexible language use. Consequently, our world language learners are often unprepared for the inherent flux and need for adaptability they will face outside the classroom, both linguistically and culturally.

Literature provides necessary practice in tolerance of ambiguity and the 'skills it takes to become knowledgeable' (Swaffar, 1998; Swaffar & Arens, 2005) in the unexpected and unpredictable. These skills will help them cope with inevitable changes (Corbett, 2003) as they move among cultures, facing challenges to become more self-directed learners. Literature provides us with opportunities for intentional engagement, a relationship involving the learner's response to this art – their experiences, perceptions and concepts and understandings within the art. Perspectives and ideas essential to a given culture can be uncovered, prompting further inquiry, change in perceptions and then transferring or transposing those ideas through formative participatory and then performance tasks. Teachers need to become facile in task design for these purposes. The late Dr Maxine Greene, Lincoln Center Institute Philosopher in Residence, spoke to these kind of experiences and believed imagination is liberated and unrestricted by our personal encounters with works of art: poetry, theatre, dance, music, fiction and visual arts. One possible lens with which to examine the work with this intention is through Aesthetic Education and the Capacities of Imaginative Learning (Lincoln Center Institute, 2008) (see Appendix A). Lincoln Center Institute (since renamed Lincoln Center Education) partners with teacher preparation programs and K-12 schools to bring teaching artists, aesthetic education workshops and performances to children and teachers in New York City and beyond.

The aesthetics of any culture, its beliefs, icons, traditions and history are essential to a culture's identity. Dr Greene affirmed that the aesthetic education 'is the intentional undertaking designed to nurture appreciative, reflective, cultural, participatory engagements with the arts by enabling learners to notice what there is to be noticed, and to lend works of art their lives in such a way that they can achieve them as variously meaningful. When this happens, new connections are made in experience: new patterns are formed, new vistas are opened'. (2001: 6). One of the goals of the aesthetic educational process is to engage teachers actively and continuously with a work of art, linking relationships between it and other human experiences, including social, historical and cultural contexts (Greene, 1995). Aesthetic Education as a method guides teachers to create these encounters for their students much like the artist design process as they create works of art (Holzer & Noppe-Brandon, 2005). When we connect to literature through drama, it enhances the capacity of the learner to construct meaning. This process allows the teacher and subsequently the language learner to explore ideas through multiple points of view (Holzer, 2005), adapt to unknowns and be flexible to them. The learner can then transfer this understanding into creating performance tasks that support the work of art, deepen inquiry into cultural practices and perspectives and explore its message through other genres.

## Reflection question

Are there cultural situations and contexts that language learners may never experience?
How do cultural perspectives inform our practices? Why are these important to understand?
How might drama enable the learner to connect with these experiences?

In *Releasing the Imagination*, Greene (1995) states,

To help kids shape their identity, we've got to awaken them to their own questions and encourage them to shape their identity, we've got to awaken them to their own questions and encourage them to create their own projects. They don't really learn unless they ask. (22)

*Essay: The Aesthetic and the Artistic in Aesthetic Education*
In this essay by Dr Maxine Greene (2009), she explores what it means to have an aesthetic experience, focusing on new possibilities and novel creations. She talks about what it means to enter the created world, the fictive world: the literary world. Greene says the work of art cannot reveal itself automatically but must be uncovered with questions. The learner must be engaged in a line of inquiry about the work and pose questions. She concludes that aesthetic education focuses on the unanswerable and leaves us with the question, Why?

*Reflections on the essay*
To what extent does aesthetic education focus on new experiences with works of art? Why do these novel connections to the work matter? How would drama nurture the 'as if' into the

created world of literature? What would the reflective encounters look like? Why does the learner need to pose questions rather than just answer questions about the work? Why is it essential for students to pose questions rather than just answer them?

# Drama for creative transfer: *One Lucky Day*

At Queens College, City University of New York, world language teachers use the Capacities for works of art in concert with the adopted performance assessment system (Adair-Hauck et al., 2003) in order to design summative and formative tasks. Teachers develop these continuous sequences of articulated tasks using the design template with components outlined in this chapter (see Appendix B). The sequence of tasks is always framed by culturally authentic material – works of art such as literature, visual and performing arts or informational texts using varied multimedia. These summative and formative assessments are part of a larger articulated, thematic, curriculum design model, Uncovering Curriculum: Assessment Design Advancing Performance to Transfer (hereafter UC:ADAPT) (Eddy, 2007, 2017), which uncovers and revisits themes over a K-16 curriculum.

## Reflection question

How does an aesthetic experience with a literary work enable creative transfer? Choose a work of literary art. What is your 'as if'?

*One Lucky Day* is a short story by Hyun Jin-geon (Hyun, 1924) set against the backdrop of Japanese occupation of Korea. The work explores themes of poverty and isolation, painful choices, conflicts, despair, denial and loss of control. These themes characterized many peoples' lives at that time, living hand to mouth just trying to survive during this colonial period. Kim is a rickshaw driver barely existing in an increasingly modern Seoul. With effects of modernity all around them, Kim and his ill wife live in impoverished conditions, barely able to sustain themselves and unable to control their general condition or their world around them. Raw, unrelenting rain and dismal colours bring the reader into Kim's life and into many other lives in this city. Kim makes the painful decision to leave his very sick wife to go to work, as she pleads that he not leave her alone. The driving rain brings him many fares for his rickshaw and so he can buy the bone broth soup his wife requested. Upon returning home, he finds her dead clutching their child. Tragic irony and universal, timeless themes are drawn from this work. Through engagement with different elements in the work, teachers and students develop sustained, participatory sequences of dramatic, creative transfer tasks (see Appendix B).

# Develop a line of inquiry

As artists create a novel work, they are in continuous engagement in order to connect with different design elements for the piece. For our purposes here with literary works of art, instructors and teachers begin this process by developing a line of inquiry (Greene, 1995; Holzer, 2005, 2007) about the literary piece. This line of inquiry integrates concepts, views, big ideas (McTighe &Wiggins, 2005) and any elements of significance derived from the work. In a classroom setting, individuals and groups all engage in this inquiry. The line of inquiry can examine a design element in a piece such as with *One Lucky Day* – cultural history, space, mood, literary techniques, people, colour, light, activity, movement, etc. Before students experience and engage the work itself, instructors develop a series of activities designed to connect students personally to it in order to guide their exploration. Over the course of the lessons and units, students create their own experiential and participatory aesthetic choices in response to the tasks. At first, they may not know what literary work they will experience. Very often, the activities and investigations may not be the same medium or genre as the literary work they will experience. This more inductive approach to the work of art is in contrast with a more deductive model of introducing the work first with demographic information on the author, reading the work, then asking the traditional, comprehension questions which allow the learner to reside in a superficial, fact-based treatment of the piece.

For developing a line of inquiry for literary works, instructors follow the process adapted from *Entering the World of the Work of Art* (Lincoln Center Institute, 2008).

1   What do you notice in the literary work? Are there any sensory elements that the author has revealed in the piece and provoked for you?
2   What questions occur to you about this piece? What are you curious about?
3   What is the cultural, historical or social backdrop or context for this work?
4   What curricular connections does this work evoke? Any personal connections?
5   What participatory and experiential tasks do you envision around this literary work?
6   Identify a list of these elements and condense to make a line of inquiry. These are the key ideas for a single line of inquiry the teacher will use to develop the tasks.

**Activity**

Choose a literary work and using the questions adapted from *Entering the World of the Work of Art,* develop a line of inquiry for the piece. You may use the literary work as well as any other artistic work that derived from the original.

## Activity

Develop the Enduring Understandings and Essential Questions that point to the line of inquiry. Make sure these address larger issues and themes in the literary work that are interdisciplinary and reprised in other contexts.

With these elements, develop the Enduring Understandings (EUs) and Essential Questions (EQs) (McTighe & Wiggins, 2005; Eddy, 2007, 2017) that will support the inclusion and implementation of this work within a curricular unit. The best EUs and EQs for world languages are drawn from intercultural perspectives that reprise and unfold across the curriculum, providing continuous engagement and serving as architecture for developing summative and then formative key performance tasks. These are big ideas and questions not limited to one literary work, unit or course but designed for sustained inquiry not only throughout the curriculum but also for the lifespan of the learner. EUs and EQs also help to preserve the integration of language in culture in curriculum, assessment and instruction, as opposed to cultural knowledge in isolation (Liddicoat & Scarino, 2010) and decontextualized linguistic skills (Byram, Gribkova & Starkey, 2002). Due to the limited scope of this chapter, it is recommended to read McTighe and Wiggins (2005) for in-depth explanation of EUs and EQs and Eddy (2007, 2017) for specific treatment and thematic unit examples in world language education.

## Example of research: Beyond drama: Post-dramatic theater in upper level, performance-oriented foreign language, literature and culture courses

Koerner (2014) explores the shift towards 'performative foreign language didactics' in drama pedagogy by adapting strategies of post-dramatic theatre techniques, placing students in the role of director, actors and authors. These strategies enhance drama pedagogy's typical treatment of characters and plot towards active production of meaning, kinaesthetic experimentation, learning by doing and creating. This study examines a German theatre course during which the author trained students with scant knowledge of theatre or drama on aesthetic activities as actors, directors and audience participants. Exercises such as detaching voice and body from language and character provided good training before encountering the work itself. Subsequent activities included creating movement and gestures, songs, scenes and scripts. Survey results indicated high levels of student engagement and an awareness that they were not inert, passive receptors of the text but active participants. They internalized a leadership role, remarking that the instructor is typically the leader in literature and culture courses. Koerner stresses that world language classes should further integrate and research performative art forms that emphasize learning by doing and embodying a work.

*Reflections on research*

*Activity*

In Koerner's study, the open-ended survey questions revealed a shift in student perception of drama and theatre works, bringing to bear the artist's decisions for the texts. Koerner speaks about identification, not with the character, but with the artist that created the work. One student wrote, 'The artist uses the medium not only to make a statement, but to pose a question.' How can the integration of these techniques enhance world language instruction and assessment practices? How do these approaches help the teacher develop a line of inquiry into the literary work for designing subsequent tasks?

# Using drama within integrated performance task design

Using the line of inquiry, the instructor designs integrated, experiential tasks for students to connect with the work. UC:ADAPT aligns the Capacities of Imaginative Learning (Holzer, 2005, 2007) (see Appendix A) with the assessment system many school districts in the United States use for assessment task design using works of art. Culturally authentic materials such as literary works are essential in designing performance-based assessment. The National Standards for Foreign Language Learning (2006), later revised as the World-Readiness Standards for Learning Languages (NSFLEP, 2014), are Communication, Culture, Connections, Comparisons, and Communities. The Communication standard is linchpin of the assessment system, comprised of the three modes of communication: interpretive, interpersonal and presentational. The four skills of listening, reading, speaking and writing previously separated and often assessed in isolation are now integrated into these three modes which more accurately demonstrate how they occur in authentic communication.

This Integrated Performance Assessment or IPA (Adair-Hauck et al., 2003) represents a cycle of the three modes centering on an overarching theme or context. The process described here is participant-driven similar to process drama (Bolton, 1979, 1992, 2003; O'Toole, 1992; O'Neill, 1995; Bolton & Heathcote, 1999; Liu, 2002; Kelin, 2009; Van Lier, 2010). The tasks are a series of integrated experiences extended over a curricular unit of study in which the ideas and responses of the literary work unfold. Each mode represents deepening engagement with the work. For our purposes in this chapter, we will look at creative task design in the three modes for the purpose of using drama for transfer. Each mode carries with it the components necessary for dramatic exploration through solving new problems, reflection and then creating new products from the original work as directors, experts, actors or spectators. The teacher presents a context as Teacher in Role, with students in flexible roles to explore different perspectives. Each IPA functions as a small drama workshop and the classroom an interactive, cultural design space, exploring relationships, sound, movement, mood, tension and meaning (Haseman & O'Toole, 1986.) In addition, IPA tasks can engage students in *metaxis* (Boal, 1995; Kingsbury-Brunetto, 2015), a state in which the learner can suspend his or her own identity to immerse more fully in the experiences of the fictional character and in post-dramatic techniques, as audience, director, author and artist (Koerner, 2014) (see Appendix B).

# Interpretive mode

The interpretive mode calls for tasks beyond traditional comprehension. As explained above, these tasks derive from the line of inquiry into the work, which eschews the low-skill-level facts fairly easy to obtain these days. In contrast, interpretive mode tasks include cultural interpretation, inference, questioning and organization of words, ideas and phrases from the culturally authentic material that learners listen to, watch or read. It is a one-way communication between the person and the piece, an opportunity to connect personally and intentionally.

In this mode, learners take ownership of the language and begin understanding with an intercultural mindset. When choosing authentic materials, it is not expected that learners understand the whole piece entirely. The task determines the level and extent and level of engagement by the learner with the work. One piece can work for all levels of instruction; it is within the design of the tasks that demonstrates what learners can do according to their level of engagement.

> ## Reflection question
>
> How do you understand the popular adage, 'Don't change the text, change the task?' When you develop the task, how do you deconstruct to the elements, even down to word or image level for the novice?

The Capacities for Imaginative learning aligned with the interpretive mode are Noticing Deeply, Embodying, Identifying Patterns and Questioning. Noticing Deeply acknowledges continuous engagement over time. Learners always come full circle to interpretive mode tasks over the course of a unit because this is where they gather information on the work or the process for engaging the literary work. The teacher also can develops tasks using varied media, visuals, music, film and prompts that enable learners to connect to personal experiences to key elements embedded in the literary text. Teachers may choose colours, music and images associated with themes in the work for this purpose. Embodying tasks in this mode ask students to physically experience the work using the senses. In the series of tasks for *One Lucky Day*, students make the shape of an object with their body, dance a drawing based on an emotional event, read aloud in different voices or emotion or create a tableau (Maley & Duff, 1978, 2005). When creating a tableau, the participants need to focus on their physical positioning, body language and facial expression. There is no speech in a tableau, and it is entirely to demonstrate understanding and embodiment of the emotion.

Categorizing and organizing images or words using a graphic organizer is an important type of interpretive mode task for Identifying Patterns. Before a learner is even at word level in the language, he or she can demonstrate comprehension with images, sounds and movements that they group into meaningful categories. Questioning is a key capacity still not fully recognized by many world language teachers. As explained earlier, typical comprehension activities involve answering questions. The interpretive mode yields more powerful results and demonstrate far better understanding when the learner poses the questions, even simple ones. The justification is thus as follows: when learners are in any real-world situation in the target language culture they will be the ones who must do the asking, therefore they need practice on questioning. Our learners do not have nearly enough opportunities to form and ask questions. They are always answering questions, particularly in typical classroom settings. One key characteristic of the intermediate level of proficiency is the ability to form questions. Therefore, forming questions should occur in the interpretive mode early and often. These activities allow the learners to engage in the dramatic process in a safe space as students use their body and senses (Piazzoli, 2011, 2014; Rothwell, 2011) to recreate, mirror and question their role and connecting to that of the artist or character. The interpretive mode coaxes the learner into facing the aesthetic question 'as if', as Maxine Greene said, of personal involvement with the work towards more noticing, movement, listening and inquiry.

> ## Sample interpretive performance assessment tasks
>
> Select an object to match the meaning of a word, phrase or entire work of art.
> Draw emotions relevant to the song or unit theme, then dance what you drew.
> Listen or watch the work and put illustrations in order.
> Gather photographs that match situation, action or themes and give them captions.

# Interpersonal mode

The learner takes the information from the interpretive mode and uses it to engage others in the interpersonal mode. The interpersonal mode is two-way, spontaneous and unscripted speaking involving negotiation of meaning. The improvisational nature of this mode lends itself quite well to using drama for exploring a work of art such as literature. This mode can occur between two or more people and involves an exchange to solve an information gap, coming to consensus, planning or decision making. The negotiation of meaning takes on particular significance in the treatment here of process drama and the ability to create their own knowledge through the drama (O'Toole, 1992). To accept different ideas and viewpoints in the tasks for *One Lucky Day*, the technique 'Yes, and …' (Farmer, 2007) asks one student to make a statement and another to listen and offer an idea, Exhibiting Empathy. The interpersonal mode adapts Forum Theatre (Boal 1982, 1992) where spectators become Spect-Actors. Anyone watching can freeze the action, taking the place of a character, halt the action and try another solution. The constant change and flux is good rehearsal for Living with Ambiguity, when the rules or patterns learners believe they know in language and culture can and will change. For 'let me ask you …' students, use the questions they developed in the interpretive mode to ask a character, author, actor or director. In this way, the learner Makes Connections to prior knowledge and those experiences of others, giving value to different perspectives that emerge from engagement with the work.

## Sample interpersonal performance assessment tasks

Propose solutions with a classmate on issues presented in work of art.
Change the time frame of the scene and improvise seconds, minutes, days or years before or after the key event occurs.
Come to consensus, plan and choose with a partner.
Create an on-air talk show that is spontaneous and unscripted.

# Presentational mode

The presentational mode consists of both spoken and written tasks intended for an audience. The best presentational mode tasks are ones which assess for transfer, when the learner can solve a novel problem or create a product, a new work of art or another piece demonstrating synthesis of learning. Given our discussion above, these should be novel problems and products, tasks that the students have not seen before that use their knowledge and skills repertoire differently than originally learned or presented.

## Sample presentational performance assessment tasks

Write a response to a character in the literary work.
Create a multimedia presentation.
Compose a different ending for the song, poem, story, novel, film, dance or play.
Create a third-person journal entry.
Draw a cartoon strip on the ideas generated from the work.
Curate a museum exhibition based on themes from the work.
Construct a game of the products, practices and perspectives of the culture.
Create a story board with words and graphics to tell story in work of art.
Write a four-line song plot for this literary work as CD liner notes.
Set the storyline in different time frames.
Write a spoof, parody or skit based on original work of art.
Be a song, literary, dance, theatre or art critic.

The drama technique, mantle of the expert (Heathcote & Herbert, 1985; Heathcote & Bolton, 1995), is applied to the design of transfer tasks in the three modes of communication (Eddy, 2007, 2014, 2017) and most appropriately in the presentational mode. The group becomes experts within the drama as planners, advisors, creators and developers in response to a context problem framed by the instructor (see Appendix B). For *One Lucky Day*, the context is to design a museum exhibit focusing on the themes in the literary work. Students at different levels of engagement can all contribute to the exhibit according to their ability, thereby differentiating tasks for an articulated treatment between levels or schools (Eddy, 2017). The tasks for *One Lucky Day* are just a sample; there are many tasks one can design for this mode. The mode engages the Capacities of Creating Meaning, Taking Action and Reflecting/Assessing. Taking Action tasks involve creating new works of art or other pieces. The tasks enable experimentation and risk-taking while connecting to the cultural perspectives through the work. These transfer tasks also allow learners to develop an awareness of their own culture, express understanding of the work in their own voice and examine common situations, emotions and issues in the work through new lenses and novel creations. This encourages and challenges the risk averse to develop empathy, flexibility and a less myopic response to cultural perspectives, values and beliefs, a key objective of intercultural competence (Fleming, 1997; Byram & Fleming, 1998; Byram, Gribkova & Starkey, 2002; Fleming, 2003).

---

## Activity

Using the Capacities for Imaginative Learning and the three modes of communication, design at least one task for each mode, keeping in mind it is a cycle of expanding depth into the work. The tasks are interdependent and each one connects to the next. The presentational mode task always solves a problem and/or creates a product as described above. Use the *One Lucky Day* exemplar as a model.

---

# Can-do statements for curriculum development and learner accountability

These tasks support the goals of can-do statements, which facilitate transparent implementation and learner autonomy. Learners are placed at the centre of the process, using can-do statements as a self-assessment tool. These can-do statements are based on the work of the *Common European Framework of Reference* (CEFR, Council of Europe, 2001), the can-do descriptors used in the *European Language Portfolio* (ELP) and the American Council on the Teaching of Foreign Languages/National Council of State Supervisors of Foreign Languages (NCSSFL/ACTFL, 2014, 2017) to describe language functions at various stages of language development and learning. Students receive can-do statements at the onset of the unit because the teachers design the assessments first in a backward design model (McTighe &Wiggins, 2005; Eddy, 2007, 2014, 2017). These specific can-do statements are different from the general unit benchmark statements set by proficiency level because teachers develop them after they created the drama tasks. Although there is just one can-do for each task in the exemplar of *One Lucky Day*, a task can certainly yield more than one can-do.

> **Activity**
>
> Derive can-do statements for each mode task. This is the learner's 'take away' and evidence. Please use the exemplar in the Appendix as a model.

# Conclusion

Drama shortens the creative distance between author and learner because these tasks engage the learner as an active participant rather than a passive consumer of the work of art or literature. Transfer tasks are intentionally creative. In order to have learners connect personally with the work, they must demonstrate an understanding of it in the context of something else or redesign it perhaps for someone else. They can do this through creative transfer tasks. By seeing the possibilities one can derive from literature or any work of art, the learner becomes less risk averse and learns to expect inherent variability and their flexible response across linguistic and intercultural experiences.

# Appendix A  The capacities for imaginative learning aligned with the three modes of communication

## Interpretive mode

**Noticing Deeply** to identify and articulate layers of detail in a work of art or other object of study through continuous interaction with it over time.

**Embodying** to experience a work of art or other object of study through your senses, as well as emotionally, and also to physically represent that experience.

**Questioning** to ask questions throughout your explorations that further your own learning; to ask the question, 'what if?'

**Identifying Patterns** to find relationships among the details that you notice, group them and recognize patterns.

## Interpersonal mode

**Making Connections** to connect what you notice and the patterns you see to your prior knowledge and experiences, to others' knowledge and experiences and to text and multimedia resources.

**Exhibiting Empathy** to respect the diverse perspectives of others in the community; to understand the experiences of others emotionally as well as intellectually.

**Living with Ambiguity** to understand that issues have more than one interpretation, that not all problems have immediate or clear-cut solutions and to be patient while a resolution becomes clear.

# Presentational mode

**Creating Meaning** to create your own interpretations based on the previous capacities, see these in the light of others in the community, create a synthesis and express it in your own voice.

**Taking Action** to act on the synthesis of what you have learned in your explorations

through a specific project. These include projects in the arts as well as in other realms. For example, you might write and produce your own play, you might create a dance, you might plant a community garden as a combined service learning/science project, you might organize a clothing drive for homeless neighbours as a combined service learning/humanities project.

**Reflecting/Assessing** to look back on your learning, continually assess what you have learned, assess/identify what challenges remain and assess/identify what further learning needs to happen. This occurs not only at the end of a learning experience but also is part of what happens throughout that experience. It is also not the end of your learning; it is part of beginning to learn something else (Holzer, 2005, 2007).

# Appendix B.

> Line of Inquiry: How does Hyun Jin-geon use imagery and language to reveal emotions, context, and irony in One Lucky Day?

**Table 3.1** One Lucky Day

> Enduring Understanding:  Loss of control may lead to painful, dilemmas and choices. Fortunate circumstances may not always lead to positive outcomes.

> Essential Question: To what extent can we control life events?  What determines our decisions? How can irony teach us life's lessons?

> Context: A museum curator needs interactive pieces for an exhibit on relationships and life's painful choices in difficult times.

| Interpretive | Interpersonal | Presentational |
|---|---|---|
| Living poetry: The instructor gives a theme or concept from the story to each small group and students write two or three words associated with that theme. Next, use the body to make an object linked to that concept. In small groups, use the movements and the associated words to create a body poem. The class guesses the theme and categorizes the words with images on a graphic organizer. For example, poverty-sad, denial, work, money, tired. | Yes, and: Using words and themes from *One Lucky Day*, the student makes a statement and their partner says Yes, and … and offers an idea. For example, I have to work. Yes, and you need money. Students come to consensus on what Kim should do that day. Using a Venn diagram, compare your choice with Kim's. | Poetry participation: Students write a poem based on *One Lucky Day* keeping the goal of dramatic irony and the unexpected in mind for a multimedia presentation. Alternatively, students can write song lyrics or rap. Using words and phrases from the work and alternative choices provided on separate cards, museum participants are invited to create their own poem as a response. |

| Interpretive | Interpersonal | Presentational |
|---|---|---|
| *I can identify and categorize words from the story.* | *I can come to consensus on choices and compare mine with the character.* | *I can create a poem and create a poetry design space.* |
| Drawing dance: Students recall an event or series of events in their life when they experienced an extreme emotion that changed quickly to an opposite emotion. Draw simple line and shapes to describe event. Use the drawing to move, using space to tell the story. | Forum Theatre: Students receive different images and scenes from the story and role play with partners using words and phrases from the story. Someone outside the group can stop the action and take the place of a character to change the outcome. | Storyboard: Design a storyboard with photos or drawings depicting scenes from *One Lucky Day*. Develop two new scenes not in the story as alternatives. Compose lines for each. Museum participants will use and recombine separate scenes to develop their own story. |
| *I can make inferences from images.* | *I can modify a story using words, phrases and emotions and continue conversation in role.* | *I can compose a story with alternative endings from multiple perspectives.* |
| Pose question: Students create still images or use those from the animated video to write single descriptive words for the images and one question to a character. | Let me ask you: In groups of four to five, each student chooses a character in the story. Each person can ask only one question to the other character in Korean. They can also ask the author. For example, 'Why did you go to work on that day?' Students write words and phrases from group on a chart. | Students create a thought tunnel by recording advice accompanied by a visual. The museum participant walks through listening to suggestions or advice, then is prompted to consider a decision. Hold a thought bubble above someone and voice the thought. |
| *I can write questions based on images and scenes.* | *I can interview a character, author or artist.* | *I can recommend choices and design an exhibit.* |

Sincere thanks and recognition to Teacher Kim Soojin Choi for sharing the history and work of Hyun Jin-geon with me.

# References

Adair-Hauck, B., E. W. Glisan, K. Koda, S. P. Sandrock and E. Swender. (2003). 'The Integrated Performance Assessment (IPA): Connecting Assessment to Instruction and Learning'. *Foreign Language Annals*, 29(3): 359–82.

Boal, A. (1982). *The Theatre of the Oppressed*. New York: Urizen Books, 1979. Republished by Routledge Press in New York/London, 1982.

Boal, A. (1992). *Games for Actors and Non-Actors*. New York: Routledge.

Boal, A. (1995). *The Rainbow of Desire: The Boal Method of Theatre and Therapy*. New York: Routledge.

Bolton, G. (1979). *Towards a Theory of Drama in Education*. London: Longman.

Bolton, G. (1992). *New Perspectives on Classroom Drama*. Great Britain: Simon & Schuster.

Bolton, G. (2003). *Dorothy Heathcote's Story: Biography of a Remarkable Drama Teacher*. Stoke on Trent, UK: Trentham Books.

Bolton, G., and D. Heathcote. (1999). *So You Want to Use Role-Play? A New Approach How to Plan*. Oakhill, UK: Trentham Books.

Byram, M., B. Gribkova, and H. Starkey. (2002). *Developing the Intercultural Dimension in Language Teaching. A Practical Introduction for Teachers*. Strasbourg: Council of Europe.

Byram, M. and M. Fleming (Eds). (1998). *Language Learning in Intercultural Perspective: Approaches Through Drama and Ethnography*. Cambridge: Cambridge University Press.

Collie, J. and S. Slater. (1996). *Literature in the Language Classroom*. Cambridge: Cambridge University Press.

Corbett, J. (2003). *An Intercultural Approach to English Language Teaching*. Clevedon: Multilingual Matters.

Council of Europe. (2001). *Common European Framework of Reference for Languages: Learning, Teaching, Assessment*. Cambridge, UK: Cambridge University Press. Available from http://www.coe.int/t/dg4/linguistic/Source/Framework_EN.pdf.

Cunico, S. (2005). 'Teaching Language and Intercultural Competence Through Drama: Some Suggestions for a Neglected Resource'. *Language Learning Journal*, 31(1): 21–9.

Eddy, J. (2007). 'Children and Art: Uncovering Cultural Practices and Perspectives Through Works of Art in World Language Performance Assessment'. *Learning Languages*, 12(2): 19–23.

Eddy, J. (2014, Spring/Summer). 'Turnarounds to Transfer: Design beyond the Modes'. *Learning Languages*, XIX(2): 16–18.

Eddy, J. (2017). 'Unpacking the Standards for Transfer: Intercultural Competence by Design'. In R. Fox (Ed.), *Special Volume on Intercultural Competence for Northeast Conference on the Teaching of Foreign Languages. NECTFL Review:* New York.

Farmer, D. (2007). *101 Drama Games and Activities*. Norwich: DramaResource.

Fleming, M. (1997). *The Art of Drama Teaching*. London: David Fulton.

Fleming, M. (2003). 'Intercultural Experience and Drama'. In G. Alred, M. Byram and M. Fleming (Eds), *Intercultural Experience and Education*, 87–100. Clevedon: Multilingual Matters.

Galloway, V. (1998). 'Constructing Cultural Realities: "Facts" and Frameworks of Association'. In J. Harper, M. Lively and M. Williams (Eds), *The Coming of Age of the Profession*, 129–40. Boston, MA: Heinle and Heinle.

Greene, M. (1995). *Releasing the Imagination: Essays on Education, the Arts, and Social Change*. San Francisco, CA: JosseyBass.

Greene, M. (2001). *Variations on a Blue Guitar: The Lincoln Center Institute Lectures on Aesthetic Education*. New York: Teachers College Press.

Greene, M. (2009). 'The Aesthetic and the Artistic in Aesthetic Education'. Retrieved 1 February 2018, from https://maxinegreene.org/library/maxine-greene-library/works-by-maxine-greene/articles.

Haseman, B. and J. O'Toole. (1986). *Dramawise: An Introduction to the Elements of Drama*. Melbourne: Heinemann.

Heathcote, D., and P. Herbert. (1985). 'A drama of learning: Mantle of the expert'. Theory Into Practice, 24(3): 173–80.

Heathcote, D. and G. Bolton. (1995). *Drama for Learning: Account of Dorothy Heathcote's 'Mantle of the Expert'*. Portsmouth, NH: Heinemann.

Holzer, M. F. (2005). *Aesthetic Education Philosophy and Practice: Education Traditions*. New York: Lincoln Center Institute.

Holzer, M. F. (2007). *Aesthetic Education, Inquiry and the Imagination*. New York: Lincoln Center Institute.

Holzer, M. and S. Noppe-Brandon (Eds). (2005). *Community in the Making: Lincoln Center Institute, the Arts, and Teacher Education*. New York: Teachers College Press.

Hyun, J. (1924). *One Lucky Day*. Translated by K. O'Rourke in *A Lucky Day* (2014), Bi-lingual Edition Modern Korean Literature, Vol. 87, Asia Publishers.

Kelin, D. A., II. (2009). *In Their Own Words: Drama with Young English Language Learners*. Charlottesville, VA: New Plays.

Kingsbury-Brunetto, K. (2015). *Performing the Art of Language Learning: Deepening the Language Learning Experience Through Theatre and Drama*. Blue Mounds, WI: Deep University Press.

Koerner, M. (2014). 'Beyond Drama: Postdramatic Theater in Upper Level, Performance-Oriented Foreign Language, Literature and Culture Courses'. Scenario, VIII(2): 4–16.

Koritz, A. (2005). 'Beyond Teaching Tolerance: Literacy Studies in a Democracy'. *Profession*, (12): 80–91.

Liddicoat, A. and A. Scarino. (2010). 'Eliciting the Intercultural in Foreign Language Education'. In L. Sercu and A. Paran (Eds), *Testing the Untestable in Language and Education*, 52–73. Clevedon: Multilingual Matters.

Lincoln Center Institute (LCI). (2008). *Entering the World of the Work of Art: A Guide for Designing an LCI Instructional Unit*. Lincoln Center for the Performing Arts. New York,

Liu, J. (2002). 'Process Drama in Second- and Foreign-Language Classrooms'. In G. Brauer (Ed.), *Body and Language: Intercultural Learning Through Drama*, 51–70. Westport, CT: Ablex.

Maley, A. and A. Duff. (1978, 2005). 'Drama Techniques: A Resource Book of Communication Activities for Language Teachers'. In P. Ur (Series Ed.), *Cambridge Handbooks for Language Teachers*, 3rd ed. Cambridge: Cambridge University Press.

McTighe, J. and G. Wiggins. (2005). *Understanding by Design*, 2nd ed. Alexandria, VA: ASCD.

Nance, K. A. (2010). *Teaching Literature in the Languages*. Boston, MA: Prentice Hall.

National Council of State Supervisors of Foreign Language. (2014). *NCSSFL-ACTFL Can-Do Statements*. ACTFL.Alexandria, VA. Revised 2017.

National Standards in Foreign Language Education Project. (2006). *Standards for Foreign Language Learning in the 21st Century*. Lawrence, KS: Allen Press.

National Standards in Foreign Language Education Project. (2014). *World-Readiness Standards for Learning Languages*. Alexandria, VA: Author.

O'Neill, C. (1995). *Drama Worlds: A Framework for Process Drama*. Portsmouth: Heinemann.

O'Toole, J. (1992). *The Process of Drama: Negotiating Art and Meaning*. London: Routledge.

Piazzoli, E. (2011). 'Process Drama: The Use of Affective Space to Reduce Language Anxiety in the Additional Language Learning Classroom'. *Research in Drama Education*, 16(4): 557–74.

Piazzoli, E. (2014). 'Engagement as Perception-in-Action in Process Drama for Teaching and Learning Italian as a Second Language'. *International Journal for Language Studies*, 8(2): 91–116.

Rothwell, J. (2011). 'Bodies and Language: Process Drama and Intercultural Language Learning in a Beginner Language Classroom. Drama Education and Second Language Learning: A Growing Field of Practice and Research'. *Research in Drama Education: The Journal of Applied Theatre and Performance*, 16(4): 575–94.

Singh, A. (2004). 'Humanising Education: Theatre in Pedagogy. Contemporary Education Dialogue'. *SAGE*, 2(1): 53–84.

Swaffar, J. (1998). 'Major Changes: The Standards Project and the New Foreign Language Curriculum'. *ADFL Bulletin*, 30(1): 34–7.

Swaffar, J. and K. Arens. (2005). *Remapping the Foreign Language Curriculum: An Approach Through Multiple Literacies*. New York: MLA, 20.

Van Lier, L. (2010). 'Agency, Self, and Identity in Language Learning'. In B. O'Rourke and L. Carson (Eds), *Language Learner Autonomy: Policy, Curriculum, Classroom*. Oxford: Peter Lang.

# 4

# The Storyline Approach and Literature

*Verna Brandford*

## Introduction

Storyline is a holistic multi-skill approach to foreign language learning and in which no skill is taught discretely. Story is a central part of the human experience. Our history, our religion, our heritage have all been passed from generation to generation through stories for thousands of years. When we seek to understand the world around us or the culture of a people, we often look to stories to enlighten us. Stories can provide children with a familiar structure and a meaningful context for learning what we are trying to teach. In this chapter, I will discuss how the Scottish Storyline method developed by in-service staff tutors Steve Bell, Sallie Harkness and Fred Rendell in 1967 at Jordanhill College of Education has the potential to use this powerful principle to teach curriculum foreign language literature content in an integrated way that closely mirrors real life.

Storylines are simulations with a narrative structure. There is a beginning, middle and an end and during the storyline; there are problems to be solved through key questions and incidents which are integral to the approach. Each Storyline has a setting, characters and a plot which includes incidents. The structure of the Storyline is planned and provided by the teacher. This comprises the introduction, the setting/place/context, the plot and a culminating event towards which the simulation progresses. The details of the Storyline are provided by the pupils, that is, the characters and the incidents.

I have chosen to draw on the work of socio-constructivist Jerome Bruner and his particular view of human thought and narrative as a theoretical model for the Storyline approach and two other socio-constructivists, Lev Vygotsky and Jean Piaget. Underpinning the theories is the importance of language in the construction of knowledge within the learner and the fact that some of the learning processes happen subconsciously in a social context. Although these processes may be facilitated by teaching and interaction, ultimately, only the learner can do it her/himself.

Storyline is an approach that is content- and context-based (Kocher, 2007) which seeks to develop fluency as well accuracy in the target language alongside the learners' developing intercultural awareness by using key questions such as, 'What do you know about French houses/apartments, schools?' Throughout the Storyline, the teacher sets tasks for the learner to use the target language in a meaningful context. The learners use and produce materials, for example ICT, video, posters, characters, word banks, collages and friezes, as they are working on a Storyline and present these to their peers and the teacher. It is the *learners* who provide the details of the Storyline which they hope will make their story interesting (Kocher, 2007: 120). It is the *teacher* who prepares the learners with the linguistic knowledge and tools necessary to work through the Storyline. Difficult issues can be naturally and safely addressed in the context of story because the situation is fictional and because the fictional situation requires attention to the issue or incident almost always chosen by the learner. The planning of activities follows on from the key questions in each new episode or part of the story. It is therefore vital that the teacher has prepared the questions in advance. These will be based on the curriculum, with opportunities for skills and cross-curricular coverage as well as differentiation. The activities clearly need to be commensurate with the linguistic levels of the learners and provide challenge.

Differentiating to meet diverse learners' needs and interests is given consideration including those pupils with special educational needs (Brandford, 2010). The original Scottish team was aware of the inclusive nature of such an approach from the earliest stages as well as the scope to develop learners' intercultural awareness. The learners create the characters and imagine the incidents that might occur in a particular theme; however they wish based on the language they have learnt, known and remembered. However, it is the teacher who paradoxically holds the thread throughout the Storyline and will guide the learners towards the conclusion or the culminating event. This will be based on her or his knowledge of the learners and their linguistic competence.

Steve Bell and Sallie Harkness, the original creators of the Storyline approach, claimed that no particular theoretical perspective influenced their work. However, there are parallels which can be drawn with the structure of the narrative form Bruner purports with that of the approach. Bruner states, 'Narrative imitates life, life imitates narrative' (Bruner, 1987: 13). He considers thought as reason, the type of thought that is prompted when constructing stories and narratives (Bruner, 1987). He applies the definition to how we talk about our lives. Underpinning this is the conviction that 'world making is the principal function of the mind' (Bruner, 1987: 11). The individual's life, according to Bruner, is constructed in a similar way to the human imagination or a narrative. We describe 'lived time … in the form of a narrative' (Bruner, 1987). This is not only a constructivist perspective but also one that underpins the Storyline approach. In taking such a position, the learners are enabled to interpret their lives and/or the knowledge they have of others' lives in any way they wish. The continuing interpretation and reinterpretation of our lives are 'ways of world making' and are part of a process of 'life making' (Bruner, 1987: 11) and is encouraged during the Storyline topics and activities. Bruner views this process as an opportunity to gain some insight into what is meant by a 'life encounter' and that recounting one's life is 'reflexive' (Bruner, 1987: 13), part of an implicit culturally construed narrative that exists in all communities.

# Storyline and socio-constructivism

The potential of the Storyline is to not only support the teaching and learning cycle and in this case, foreign languages but also to provide the opportunity to forge learner–teacher relationships and activate the learner's cognitive and meta-cognitive skills through semi-authentic and communicative language tasks which might engage, motivate and aid their progress. A sociocultural and constructivist framework is presented to the learners for 'authentic communication' to take place. 'Language is regarded as a means of communication' (Kocher, 2007: 122). Through the four language skills of listening, speaking, reading and writing, the learners have opportunities to interact with each other, for example, through the characters and communicate ideas which Kocher states can create an 'information gap' and 'give a reason for meaningful and purposeful communication' (Kocher, 2007).

A distinctive element of the Storyline approach is the opportunities organized during each episode for the learner to assume the personal traits of the character created throughout the Storyline topic, for example, La Pluie in Le petit Nicolas et les copains (Sempé and Goscinny, 1963).

To give further credence to this view, Bruner uses the example of Sartre who writes in his autobiography, 'A man is always a teller of stories, he lives surrounded by his own stories and those of other people, he sees everything that happens to him in terms of these stories and he tries to live his life as if he were recounting it'(Sartre, 1964). Stories according to Bruner do not 'just happen in the head but happen to people' giving rise to 'reinterpretation of experiences' and 'selective recall' (Bruner, 1987: 12–13). He views the narrator (self) and the key character as one and the same. He continues that self-narratives can pose problems as they are almost always unverifiable and 'beyond rationalization' (Bruner, 1987). While this might be the case, Bruner suggests that demanding 'internal criteria' are at play which are based on what the narrator/key character felt or intended. Consequently, the narrative accounts that ensue are also 'susceptible to cultural, interpersonal and linguistic influences which have the potential to change someone's life narrative' (Bruner, 1997: 15). These are significant points as the Storyline would appear to afford the learner the choice and decision-making opportunities he or she wishes to share about his or her lives through the characters and incidents without being subjected to any verification in terms of what has or has not been included (Bruner, 1987).

Language clearly plays a significant role as it 'constructs what it narrates – semantically, pragmatically and stylistically' and can facilitate the narrator to 'make the ordinary, strange' (Bruner, 1987: 17). A good example is the range of Storyline characters created by the learners.

The opportunities to incorporate different genres or 'set of grammars' (Bruner, 1987: 17) when designing a Storyline topic are not so obvious in a course book or syllabus and serve to not only reinforce concepts initially learned in English lessons but to also build on knowledge of the target language and related communities which can now be revisited or taught and used in different contexts according to the setting, plot, characters and incidents.

Due to the constructed nature of life narratives and the extent to which they might adhere to 'cultural conventions' and 'language usage' (Bruner, 1987), they are inevitably influenced and are part of one's culture. Bruner refers to a tool kit of 'canonical life narratives', for example, heroes, villains, tricksters and so on, specific to each culture with which everyone is familiar such as the moralistic Jamaican Anansi stories, Aesop's fables and so on which are endemic in all cultures and from which citizens might construct or model their own life narratives (Bruner, 1987). Bruner highlights the powerful influence of the tool kit 'to structure perceptual experience' (Bruner, 1987: 15) and by implication to become the narrative that we as individuals recount. He writes that 'variants of the canonical forms' can enable the transmission of a particular culture which ultimately takes control of one's life. Linked to this, he discusses the notion of 'how our way of telling about ourselves changes'. Bruner takes the view that while we sometimes commit 'breaches of the canonical' which despite being influenced by narrative traditions can 'also provide rich grounds for innovation' (Bruner, 1991). This perspective captures the dynamic nature of culture and its related reference points (Brandford, 2010). It was precisely this sense of change and unconventionality which appealed when considering opportunities for the pupils to use their imagination and creativity to say what they wanted to say or write in the target language. The Storyline approach appeared to offer those creative opportunities.

However, there are elements of this view of narratives worth considering in relation to the learner's linguistic and intercultural development during a Storyline topic including the following:

The extent to which the learners are required to assume the identity of a character based on the implicit cultural form or tool kit as referred to by Bruner, of the target language speaking community with which they may have varying degrees of familiarity and knowledge. How important is this?

Is the focus on the language or the cultural knowledge demonstrated by the learner or both?

I take the view that depending on the age and stage of the learner, the primary focus during a Storyline topic in modern foreign languages would be on linguistic development without downplaying the inextricable link with intercultural understanding. The concepts of self-narrative suggested by Bruner appear more universal than peculiar to a given culture and variations could be compared when using authentic resources from the target language–speaking communities with the learners. Bruner acknowledges this universality and states that variations will include those of a linguistic as well as those of a cultural nature in terms of how the narrative form is expressed (Bruner, 1997).

Bruner's narrative structure based on the work of Vladimir Propp and Burke presents further interesting parallels with that of a Storyline topic (see Table 4.1 below).

While the structure suggested by Bruner in Table 4.1 is not a direct match to that of the Storyline approach, the basic elements of the 'setting', 'agent'-'character', 'trouble'-'incident' are evident,

**Table 4.1** Parallels between Bruner's Narrative Structure and the Storyline Approach

| Bruner's suggested narrative structure | Storyline approach |
| --- | --- |
| Agent | Character |
| Goal | Plot/character |
| Setting | Place |
| Instrument | Character |
| Trouble | Incident |

I would argue that 'goal' and 'instrument' are aspects implicit in the character's role and are driven by the manner in which the characters respond to the incidents.

Interestingly, Bruner concludes by suggesting that it is through our experiences when encountering 'trouble' that we construct a self for the future based on memories of how we coped. The tasks devised by the teachers using the Storyline approach are nothing new; what is different to the routine foreign language classroom activity is 'the idea of using narrative contexts to provide a supportive structure for both learners and teachers' (Bell, 2007). Such engagement enables learners to consider imaginative or feasible real-life possibilities with the 'instruments' at their disposal to achieve their 'goal' as they resolve 'trouble' through the character they have created.

## Window of research

### The narrative construction of reality

Bruner writes of the quest to discover how we achieve 'reality' of the world and subsequently respond to it. This view of narrative is not without opposing views. He makes the point that most knowledge that we have about 'reality constructing' emanates from what we know about the natural and physical world as opposed to the 'human or symbolic' world. We still know very little about the social world and how we construct and represent human interaction. Bruner writes that there are principles and procedures in the way we go about constructing each domain of the world and that these are influenced by a 'cultural toolkit' or 'tradition' and that we organize our experiences and what we remember involving ourselves and others in the form of narrative – a version of reality.

For further reading on this topic, please see link below. Bruner's prime focus in the article that follows explores the notion of how narrative 'operates as an instrument of the mind as we construct reality'. He suggests ten significant features of the narrative form.

http://www.jstor.org/stable/1343711

## Vygotsky and Storyline

If we turn briefly to the work of social constructivist, Lev Vygotsky, learning is seen to take place in, what he termed, the zone of proximal development (ZPD) (Vygotsky, 1978). The ZPD can be viewed as where what is learned follows on from subject matter that has already been learned. For the learner, it is something new that he or she was unable to do previously with a more competent other, for example, a peer, teacher and then after working with this individual/individuals or 'a dialectical exchange' (Wrigley, 2007: 48), the learner is then able to complete the task unaided. This was later termed 'scaffolding' by Bruner in his research on culture in education where learning is perceived as a process of interaction (Bruner, 1996). There is significant overlapping between the two theorists in relation to the role of language which Vygotsky views as a crucial element of the learning context and how the learner can through language use become part of the culture and subsequently, a citizen. Key to the role is the relationship with thinking and language considered as a 'social tool for thinking' (Wrigley, 2007: 48).

# Piaget and Storyline

Piaget was also interested in what happened inside the learner's mind that could not be observed or measured. Like Vygotsky, he was aware of the experience and knowledge capital that the learner brings to the classroom. This capital was perceived as forming a cognitive framework of 'structures' within which the learner links new experiences and knowledge to those already in place. He termed this process 'assimilation' that is subject to frequent adaptation in order to make more links possible – 'accommodation' (Piaget, 1937).

As Wrigley reports on the similarities between the theorists when writing about learning theory and the Storyline approach, these are that they 'all support the view of learning as an individual and subjective construction that happens when one is actively engaged in learning and that the learning process is facilitated by being in a social context' (Wrigley, 2007: 50).

The Storyline approach is learner-centred and is reliant on the learner's experiences and previous knowledge from the earliest stages of the language learning process. While the teacher is instrumental in moving the story forward, learning is privileged over teaching and is 'experiential' as the learners 'situate themselves within the narrative' playing the characters (Wrigley, 2007: 169). This study takes the sociocultural view that integral to the Storyline approach is the interaction and use of language that takes place between individuals. Inherent in the sociocultural constructivist perspective is the notion of any change or difference occurring as learners 'gain control of and reorganize their cognitive processes during mediation as knowledge is internalised during social activity' (Lightbown & Spada, 2006: 47). Lantolf and Thorne, also socio-constructivists, write that one of the benefits of a sociocultural approach to SLA research such as that of the Storyline is that 'it offers a framework through which cognition can be investigated without isolating it from social context' (Lantolf & Thorne, 2006: 19). The learner has the opportunity to demonstrate knowledge and understanding in the Storyline foreign language classroom as the character created in a given topic setting, for example, La Pluie set in a school classroom.

This concept of language as a social tool to be acquired and used in a social setting (Atkinson, 2002) finds its origins in the work of Lev Vygotsky and the prioritization of interaction in his theory of the mind (Vygotsky, 1978). An interesting and more inclusive definition of Vygotsky's ZPD is posited by Wells who perceives the model as 'an interactive space that holds the potential for multiple – unpredictable – transformations of individual identity' (Wells & Claxton, 2002). This definition allows all learners to demonstrate particular talents and skills in different and valorized ways as they proceed through the Storyline episodes, for example, drama, art, music, dance and as tools for their thinking and communication. From a sociocultural perspective as suggested above, the opportunity to focus on the learners as they engage in and comment on tasks has the potential to develop understanding of the learning process (Donato, 2000). Storyline is a task-based approach but as Lantolf writes, it is the importance of the individual's interaction with the task (Lantolf, 2000) and the evaluation afterwards that will yield useful data and contribute to that understanding. However, the planning and design process is also required to encourage pupil ownership and with that acceptance of the direction in which the learners wish to take the Storyline as their fictional characters and the incidents.

# Teaching a Storyline

After deciding what the students need to learn or revise, the teacher chooses a setting or context appropriate to the intended learning outcomes. The teacher then plans learning experiences around typical story elements such as incidents which the students may choose involving issues of security, personal health and well-being or issues of good and evil, etc. As the teacher continues developing the Storyline, real life and plausible episodes are planned which are not unlike chapters in a novel. These episodes are intended to give logical meaning to the subject matter content.

A Storyline structure described below might take one lesson to two weeks or longer. Elements of the Storyline might be used as a way to revisit and revise previously learnt lexis/structures, for example, the creation of the characters, incidents, culminating event.

**Selection of a theme** – This is connected to the theme from the curriculum. The teacher uses the theme to generate ideas for the Storyline. When selecting a Storyline, consideration has to be given not only to the curriculum but also to the level of target language use by the learners and the assessment requirements in place. Grammatical accuracy and use of the target language are not downplayed and must be monitored by the teacher. Both elements are pursued with the same rigour and consistency as the teacher continues to judiciously select and sequence subject matter when planning, to ensure that the teaching and learning objectives are achievable and that the pupils are making progress in their language learning.

It is necessary to find a context in which the desired knowledge will make sense – a point that resonates with the foreign language teacher, for example, when planning to introduce and practise new grammatical structures or items. The teacher is guided by the pupils' needs and interests, curriculum, scheme of work, the course book, examination specifications and possible cross-curricular/cultural /real-life opportunities.

**Clear teaching objectives and learning outcomes** – The teacher should be clear as to the purpose of the Storyline and how it will benefit the learners and their progress. It may be that the teacher revisits previous learning such as the past tense in a new context and in more breadth and depth. S/he may decide to introduce a new topic through a Storyline such as 'La Pluie' (below). The learning outcomes are decided in advance with possible episodes of the Storyline. In most stories, the format is familiar to the learner. The Storyline is just one 'way of delivering the required curriculum' (Harkness, 2006a).

**Key questions** – The episodes are the threads running through each Storyline (Bell, 2000: 3). The story elements of the setting, characters and plot serve as both a planning model and as a pedagogical approach (Letschert et al., 2006). These episodes are intended to give logical meaning to the subject matter content. The development of other skills is also encouraged such as collaboration, empathy and respect. The pupils usually want to find out about the characters that their peers have created and talk about their own. My observations of Storyline teaching and learning, feedback as well as my involvement in workshops over the past fifteen years would suggest that learners in all phases including adults want to interact, speak, listen and use the dictionary to find words to express what *they* want to say. Learning a language is after all a social activity.

The episodes are sequenced by key questions which structure the learning during the Storyline (Krenicky-Albert, 2004: 7). Consideration will need to be given to the related key questions which will develop the sequence of the Storyline and encourage activities which allow the learners to demonstrate their knowledge and understanding and support the development of skills as well as their ideas in the target language. Because the learners have created the human element in the visual characters, they usually develop a personal investment in the narrative which develops in the learners exploring not only the factual answers to questions but also the subjective feelings, moral values and implications of actions (Bell & Harkness, 2006). It is a holistic, learner-centred, topic-oriented and cross-curricular approach which encourages co-operative and collaborative experiential learning, that is, learning by doing (Kocher, 2007).

**Organization of resources** – The use of basic and, if appropriate, authentic and accessible material is crucial to the success of the Storyline. These would include dictionaries to build on previously learnt lexis, word bank sheets to share new lexis with peers, magazines and newspapers to create the characters, artefacts, written work from previous Storylines/lessons and access to the internet and other sources for research purposes. Competent dictionary use is crucial. Dictionary skills must be taught or revisited as learners are encouraged to make use of, add to, create and refer to their own 'word banks' which are displayed as they progress through the Storyline for the class to see and use.

Classroom organization and resources are standard considerations at the planning stage of any teaching and learning episode and should facilitate the teacher to vary the groupings appropriately.

## Storyline structure with La Pluie in Le Petit Nicolas et les copains –Tasks to do in class

The literary extract 'La Pluie' from the 'Le petit Nicolas' series of books has been selected to illustrate how this principle might be implemented in the foreign languages classroom.

A typical structure of a Storyline will have the following components:

*an introduction,*
*a setting,*
*characters,*
*incidents*
*and a culminating event*

These will be explained in more detail in the example below.

Aspects of anticipation and curiosity are key to any story as most pupils will want to know, 'What is going to happen next?' following each episode and are interested to see where it will develop. Anticipation can ensure that learning continues whether in school or at home because the pupils are involved in a process that they feel a part of (Cresswell, 1997).

The critical partnership between teacher and pupil in a Storyline topic often becomes a more collaborative storymaking venture because of the potential for balance of control between the two parties. The teacher leads at all times holding the thread which is the 'storyline' planned and is informed by the curriculum (Cresswell, 1997).

Storyline topics start with key questions and start by building the pupils' conceptual model first and finding out what they already know. For example, 'Qu'est-ce que c'est qu'un(e)_____?' or 'C'est comment un(e)_____?'

I start from the premise that learners build their understanding by going from the known to the unknown. A context such as that of a Storyline topic can motivate children to learn by providing a real-life scenario that is familiar, in this case, pupils having to stay in the classroom because of the poor weather. In a modern foreign language context, pupils often want to search the dictionary in order to practise reading, speaking, writing and listening skills and assimilate new subject matter because the story requires it and because they have something they want to communicate. As a revision vehicle, the Storyline topic can facilitate the pupils' participation and contributions as they revisit previous learning and build on what they already know (Cresswell, 1997).

In the Storyline example, *La Pluie* below, each aspect of the structure outlined above is incorporated and exemplified. The extract is used as an initial stimulus for the Storyline language learning activities that will proceed. The setting is the school classroom of the main character and remains constant throughout this particular Storyline topic and the culminating event. (See Table 4.2 for a suggested template for planning.)

a.   The **introduction** to the Storyline is teacher-led. The teacher introduces the topic, La Pluie, with a stimulus related to the topic and which might be of interest to the learners: the text, photos/images of rain or different weather conditions or video clips from the cartoon. The text could be broken down to be read as extracts in lessons or for homework with comprehension tasks to familiarize them with the content and to prepare them for the Storyline topic activities that follow. The teacher might omit parts of the text to combine with Storyline-type activities, for example, the concluding paragraphs of the chapter. Having read the text, the class discusses in the target language which weather conditions they like and give reasons – discussing their own preferences and what they can understand in the text extract. The teacher could then show weather forecasts from sources such as newspapers and the internet to encourage pupils to look for similarities and differences when compared with reasons for school closure in Britain not only based on the images conveyed in the text. The learners could then describe (and draw) their ideal weather conditions or could be encouraged to revisit previous learning, the text and the dictionary for support. This first episode (or chapter) would be establishing the setting and asking the pupils what they know and want in a particular setting. Revision content could also include what they wear in certain weather conditions.

b.   **Characters** – After the setting, the focus is on the people involved – the characters which are created by the learners. These can be created collaboratively or individually based on the descriptions of Nicolas' friends. The characters can be drawn, made from clay, magazine pages, lollipop sticks, Avatars and have biographies usually based on a template for support and for which the pupils have the option to extend on their own and ideas from their peers as well as using the dictionary. The biographies are usually written in narrative or note form at the back of each character and include personality traits. The notes serve as prompts for each learner or group as they talk about themselves as the character and when they meet another character. These characters can be as conventional as the learners wish them to be in terms of physical appearance, personality traits, dress and biographies.

c.   **Plot** – The teacher then introduces the plot, for example, what happens in school during adverse weather conditions. The learners then decide who the characters are, in this case, friends of Nicolas. It is usual for each learner to become a character or in some cases, in small groups, they work collaboratively and create one character to present. The characters meet – there is some interaction. For example, in the Storyline, La Pluie, the characters introduce and organize themselves in friendship groups for the break or lunch time and discuss what they intend to do together. There is an opportunity here for pupils to share actual and imaginary weather conditions and codes of conduct/rules that exist or that they wish to invent. The learners act out their characters according to their biographies. It is at this point during one of the breaks that an incident happens. The learners decide which incidents will happen during the Storyline. It is usually one major incident. The pupils decide which incident in discussion as a whole class after reading what happens in La Pluie or what they decide will happen with the teacher taking on the role as arbitrator. The plot then develops through asking key questions which derive from the characters interacting within the school setting and based on previous knowledge and experiences. The learner is invited to be involved in forming the plot by the teacher asking, 'Qu'est-ce qui va se passer à …?' These incidents could be either positive or negative occurrences which require problem solving (Emo, 2010). The teacher will have in mind possible incidents, for example, fire, burglary, homework theft and so on, but it is considered good practice for the learners to suggest their own. The incidents are the 'bedrock of a successful Storyline' (Emo, 2007: 23). The learners decide on how their characters will respond to the incidents that they encounter often drawing or building on previous subject matter learnt or modifying aspects of the text.

d.   **Culminating Activity** – A school assembly takes place and the hero/heroine pupil (character) who resolved the incident is celebrated, or a manifesto for code of conduct for pupils and staff during adverse weather conditions is shared with the whole school.

Most Storyline topics are planned and delivered in a similar way to the structure outlined above. Within each of the four episodes, the flexibility of the approach affords the learners the opportunities to create further details relating to their interests, experiences, imagination and creativity for example:

the setting and location – the use of authentic names found on the internet;

the inclusion of different objects/pets/toys etc. one of the characters might be an animal;

the incident could be as challenging as the learners want it to be and could be responded to in different and creative ways, or as Wrigley prefers to describe it, 'a particular medium or genre of learner activity' including drama, writing, art and research (Wrigley, 2007: 169);

The culminating event should always be a gathering or plenary of some sort with an intended audience to view/hear what has been produced by the learners during the Storyline. These might be for example, friezes, pictures, characters, photos, writing, video clips, a radio broadcast and so on.

# Conclusion

The Storyline approach by its very nature provides numerous opportunities to make links with authentic literature with a view to supporting and developing linguistic competence and interculturality. As a teaching and revision vehicle, the approach complements the use of extracts or chapters such as La Pluie. Using literature in this way can help to provide real-life and relevant contexts to engage, motivate and encourage the pupils to actively participate and interact during lessons to use the target language creatively and say what *they* wish to say.

**Table 4.2** Storyline Planning Template

## La Pluie

# Episode 1

| Storyline | Key questions | Teacher activity | Pupil activity | Material | Outcome/ assessment | Skill |
|---|---|---|---|---|---|---|
| La Pluie | **Based on the text:** | Organize reading activities focussed on the text in class/as homework activity | Pupils in pairs/ groups matching, multiple choice, translating | Authentic text Graded worksheet | Complete the order of events in the text | **Reading Writing** |
| | Qu'est-ce que c'est que la pluie? Qu'est-ce tu fais quand il pleut/il neige/il fait froid/ il fait chaud à l'école? | Teacher asks the questions | Whole-class activities: reading aloud parts of the text, true/false team game | Text | Pupils respond to questions and justify their responses | **Reading Speaking** |
| | Tu aimes la pluie/ la neige/le froid/ la chaleur? /Quel temps préfères-tu? Pourquoi? Quel temps fait-il à…? Quel est le temps idéal pour toi? Qu'est-ce qui se passe/ s'est passé? C'est vrai/faux? | | | | | |

# Episode 2

| Storyline | Key questions | Teacher activity | Pupil activity | Material | Outcome/ assessment | Skill |
|---|---|---|---|---|---|---|
| Les élèves | Qui est dans ta classe? Comment est-il/elle? | Asks the questions Facilitates and circulates | Create characters in pairs/groups/ individually either based on those in the text or create their own | Biography template, dictionaries, art materials, access to the internet | Write biographies for their characters (for display) | **Writing** |
| | | Circulates and monitors | Pupils circulate taking on the role of the character they have created. The character asks and responds to questions | Character biography templates for note-taking | Templates are completed with details about the new character(s) (for display) | **Listening Speaking Writing** |
| | | Organizes timing of group interaction | He or she makes notes about the other characters they meet | | | |
| | Qui est ton copain/ta copine? Pourquoi? | Asks the question | Whole-class activity Pupils share with the rest of the class which character has been chosen as a friend and give the reason for their choice | | Notes taken are used to describe the character who has to with the rest of the class guess who is being described. Justifying choice | **Speaking Listening Reading** |

# Episode 3

| Storyline | Key questions | Teacher activity | Pupil activity | Material | Outcome/ assessment | Skill |
|---|---|---|---|---|---|---|
| Le temps | Quel temps fait-il maintenant? | Asks the questions | In groups pupils plan, write and present the adverse weather conditions they have chosen Whole-class activity. The rest of the class listen and write the weather conditions heard | Dictionaries | Present their weather announcements | **Speaking Listening Writing** |
| | Qu'est-ce qu'il faut faire quand il . . .? | Facilitates and monitors | | | | |
| | | Organizes the running dictation activity for each group | Pupils remain in groups and decide what the school rules are for the adverse weather conditions. These are displayed. Whole-class activity | Flipchart paper | The rules constitute the content of the running dictation for another group | **Reading Speaking Listening Writing** |
| | Qu'est-ce qui va se passer à… | Asks the question Suggests incidents | Whole-class activity. Pupils suggest incidents. An incident is agreed | Storyboard templates | Pupils draw a comic strip of the incident with speech balloons/ narrative (for display) | **Writing Drawing** |
| | Qu'est-ce qui s'est passé? Qui a trouvé la solution? | Asks the questions | In groups, pupils write and rehearse a short telephone conversation with a parent describing what the incident was and explain how the incident was resolved and by whom | Props, recording equipment | Conversations are audio-recorded for assessment | **Writing Speaking** |

## Episode 4

| Storyline | Key questions | Teacher activity | Pupil activity | Material | Outcome/assessment | Skill |
|---|---|---|---|---|---|---|
| La présentation de nouvelles règles aux parents et aux professeurs | Quelles sont les règles maintenant à l'école quand il fait très mauvais? | Asks the question<br><br>Facilitates | In groups, pupils prepare and present the new rules | Paper | Presentation of the new rules which are displayed and voted on by the other groups | **Speaking Writing Reading** |
| | | Arbitrator | The groups listen to each presentation and read the rules on display. They cast a vote for the best rules | | The rules with the most votes are displayed around the school | **Listening Reading Writing** |

### Reflections

When considering the use of literature, how might the 'breaches of the canonical' referred to by Bruner support the notion of innovation and yet also maintain cultural relevance for pupils in the foreign language classroom? How could the Storyline approach play a role?

What is inherently distinctive and different about the Storyline approach and which nevertheless enables it to be part of the foreign language teaching and learning process?

# References

Atkinson, D. (2002). 'Toward a Sociocognitive Approach to Second Language Acquisition'. *Modern Language Journal*, 86(iv): 25–45.

Bell, S. (2000). 'Storyline, Feelings, and Respect'. In E. Hakonsson (Ed.), *The International Storyline Conference*, 5–12. Aalborg: The Royal Danish School of Education.

Bell, S. (2007). 'Continuing Professional Development in Storyline'. In S. Bell, S. Harkness and G. White (Eds), *Storyline – Past, Present and Future*, 27–32. Glasgow: Enterprising Careers.

Bell, S. and S. Harkness. (2006). *Storyline: Promoting Language across the Curriculum*. Royston: UKLA.

Brandford, V. (2010). 'Preparing for Diversity'. In R. Heilbronn and J. Yandell (Eds), *Critical Practice in Teacher Education: A Study of Professional Learning*. London: Institute of Education.

Bruner, J. (1987). 'Life as Narrative in Social Research'. *Reflections on Self*, 54(1), 11–32.

Bruner, J. (1991, Autumn). 'The Narrative Construction of Reality'. *Critical Inquiry*, 18: 1–21.

Bruner, J. (1996). *The Culture of Education*. Cambridge, MA: Harvard University Press.

Bruner, J. (1997). 'A Narrative Model of Self-Construction'. *Annals of the New York Academy of Sciences*, 818: 145–61.

Cresswell, J. (1997). *Creative Worlds*. Portsmouth, NH: Heineman.

Donato, R. (2000). 'Sociocultural Contributions to Understanding the Foreign and Second Language Classroom'. In J. Lantolf (Ed.), *Sociocultural Theory and Second Language Learning*. Oxford: Oxford University Press.

Emo, W. (2010). *Teachers Who Initiate Curriculum Innovation: Motivations and Benefits*. Doctoral thesis, University of York.

Harkness, S. (2006a). 'Storyline – An Approach to Effective Teaching and Learning'. In S. Bell, S. Harkness and G. White (Eds), *Storyline – Past, Present & Future*. Glasgow: University of Strathclyde.

Harkness, S. (2006b). 'Examples of Storyline Topic Outlines – 1'. In S. Bell, S. Harkness and G. White (Eds), *Storyline – Past, Present and Future*, 118–24. Glasgow: Enterprising Careers.

Krenicky-Albert, K. (2004). *Project Work, Cross-Curricular or Interdisciplinary Teaching and Learning – Storyline as an Approach to Effective Foreign Language Teaching*. Seminar Paper. Norderstedt, Germany: GRIN.

Kocher, D. (2007). 'Why Storyline Is a Powerful Tool in the Foreign Language Classroom'. In S. Bell, S. Harkness and G. White (Eds), *Storyline – Past, Present and Future*, 118–24. Glasgow: Enterprising Careers.

Lantolf, J. (2000). 'Second Language Learning as a Mediated Process'. *Language Teaching*, 33: 79–96.

Lantolf, J. P. and S. Thorne. (2006). *Sociocultural Theory and the Genesis of Second Language Development*. Oxford: Oxford University Press.

Letschert, J., B. Grabbe-Letschert and J. Greven. (2006). *Beyond Storyline: Features, Principles and Pedagogical Profundity*. Enschede: SLO.

Lightbown, P. and N. Spada. (2006). *How Languages Are Learned*, 3rd ed. Oxford: Oxford University Press, 47.

Piaget, J. (1937). *La naissance de l'intelligence, la construction du reel chez l'enfant et la formation du symbole chez l'enfant*, Paris De la chaux et Niestlé.

Sartre, J-P. (1964). *The Words*. New York: Braziller.

Sempé, J.-J. and R. Goscinny. (1963). *Le petit Nicolas et les copains*. Gallimard.

Vygotsky, L. (1978). *Mind in Society*. Cambridge, MA: Harvard University Press.

Wells, G. and G. Claxton. (2002). 'Introduction: Sociocultural Perspectives on the Future of Education'. In G. Wells and G. Claxton (Eds), *Learning for Life in the 21st Century: Sociocultural Perspectives on the Future of Education*. Malden, MA: Blackwell.

Wrigley, T. (2007). *Projects, Stories, and Challenges: More Open Architectures for School Learning In: Storyline – Past, Present and Future*. Glasgow: Enterprising Careers, 118–24.

# 5

# Literature in Non-European Languages

*Frances Weightman*

## Introduction

Chinese is not an easy language to master.

Whenever debates on the expansion of Chinese in our secondary schools hit the headlines, the difficulty or otherwise of the language seems almost to become an obsession with journalists, politicians, parents and bloggers.[1] Some critics suggest that we are wasting our time, and our resources, teaching Chinese to English native speakers when other foreign languages are so much more accessible – why set our young people up to fail? This controversy seems particularly acute in the UK, where, as I detail below, there are fairly some dramatic changes in Chinese language provision taking place at the school level. I feel these discussions sometimes miss the point: of course, it takes time to become completely proficient in Chinese, but it also takes time to become a nuclear physicist – no one suggests we should not include physics in the secondary curriculum. It's the process that matters, and the understanding of some basic concepts, not the finished product.

But given the evident anxiety that surrounds the introduction of this language into the school curriculum, is it simply foolhardy to go further and try to incorporate literary texts into what we teach, rather than focussing purely on practical communicative skills? Is the study of Chinese literature an ornamental extra which should remain the preserve of university departments and retired amateur sinologists?

The University of Leeds in the UK runs a project called 'Writing Chinese' which is all about showcasing contemporary Chinese writing and exploring its reception in the West. We have been looking at a wide range of authors, considering their reception on the global stage, focussing mainly on those appearing for the first time in English translation. We've featured several very controversial new writers, dealing with topics that are often very 'adult' in nature, in an attempt to showcase the huge range of writing produced in China today (more than just classics and Cultural Revolution memoirs). We regularly use these texts in our undergraduate teaching as well as in our research. But, if we are to truly attempt to evaluate the ability of literature to pass from one cultural milieu to another, however, perhaps the litmus test is whether or not a story written for children and teenagers in one country 'works' for children in another. And, as with so many things, the crux of this is presentation.

Rather than adding to any perceived inaccessibility of the Chinese language, in what follows I suggest that the careful incorporation of the study of selected literary texts into your curriculum can in fact help pupils appreciate both the linguistic context and the broader cultural background of their language learning. Taught sensitively, the study of Chinese literature, whether in the original language or in translation, can be intensely motivating and intellectual stimulating as well as providing excellent opportunities for classroom debates and cross-cultural understanding.

# Context

Chinese teaching in UK schools recently received a significant boost, with the announcement in 2016 of a £10 million investment by the UK government in the Mandarin Excellence Programme, providing intensive teaching of Chinese (eight hours per week) to 5,000 school pupils across England and Wales. As this programme develops, it is anticipated that the study of Chinese language and culture will be embedded across the curriculum in schools throughout the UK.

At the same time as this increasing presence of Chinese in the UK school curriculum, the nature of what is taught is also shifting away from 'textbook' dialogues. In September 2013, the UK Department for Education produced new National Curriculum guidelines for the study of languages at primary and secondary schools, placing new emphasis on the study of literary texts within the curriculum.[2] The introductory 'Purpose of Study' of the new National Curriculum states that one of the aims of teaching of foreign languages should be to give pupils opportunities to 'read great literature in the original language'. Further, pupils should 'discover and develop an appreciation of a range of writing in the language studied'. At key stage 2, pupils should be taught 'to appreciate stories, songs, poems and rhymes in the language', while by key stage 3 (11–14 year olds) they should be able to 'read literary texts in the language [such as stories, songs, poems and letters], to stimulate ideas, develop creative expression and expand understanding of the language and culture'.

The GCSE and A-level specifications for Chinese are being prepared according to the models and targets established for European languages. Specifically, at GCSE level (14–16 year olds) in reading, to 'recognise and respond to key information, important themes and ideas in more extended written text and authentic sources, including some extracts from relevant abridged or adapted literary texts'[3] and at AS and A2 levels (16–19 year olds) to 'engage critically with intellectually stimulating texts, films and other materials in the original language, developing an appreciation of sophisticated and creative uses of the language and understanding them within their cultural and social context'.[4]

The new specifications for AS and A2 levels must enable students to develop their language by a range of means, including 'reading and responding to a variety of texts including some extended texts written for different purposes and audiences drawn from a range of authentic sources, including contemporary, historical and literary, fiction and non-fiction texts, adapted as necessary'. At AS level, students must also study one literary work or film in depth and 'include a critical response to aspects such as the structure of the plot, characterisation, and use of imagery or other stylistic features, as appropriate to the work studied'. At A2, specifications require students to study either one or two literary works, which 'must include a range from at least two of the following genres: novels, series of short stories, plays, selections of poems, life writing (such as autobiography, biography, letters and journals)'.[5]

Insisting that the syllabus for Chinese mirrors that for European languages, and on the need to incorporate 'literary texts', is a cause for concern for many. After the publication of these guidelines, the Writing Chinese project conducted a survey at the 2015 Chinese Teachers Conference[6] hosted by the Institute of Education, London, to gauge the reaction of school teachers to the idea of including literature within their teaching. Unsurprisingly, the vast majority of teachers told us that they felt underprepared and apprehensive. Literature, for these teachers, whether Chinese nationals or UK-trained, meant the great classical works – and how could these be adequately abridged or simplified to an appropriate level of language for the pupils they were teaching? Texts, everyone agreed, needed to be available in English translation, regardless of whether they are being taught for language or content.

## Why teach Chinese literature?

Despite the understandable anxiety around teaching literature, and regardless of views on these kind of curriculum guidelines, which are by their nature both necessarily prescriptive and temporary, there are also many sound reasons for teaching Chinese literature. Working in a university department that traditionally favoured contemporary social sciences over the humanities, and facing the usual budgetary pressures and market-led curriculum common to all HE institutions, I have frequently needed to make the case for the vital importance of the study of literature within a language programme. Some of these principles are of course common to all languages, but I would argue that in the Chinese case there are specific incentives that transcend any initial concerns.

## As inspiration and motivation for students

With the best will, teaching materials and the most committed and enthusiastic students in the world, learning Chinese characters can be a very dull process. The initial excitement of producing your first attempt at the script, perhaps slowly with calligraphy brushes in a Chinese taster day, soon fades. As China and Chinese culture becomes an increasingly pervasive influence in Western society, any perceived 'exoticism' is quickly disappearing. With the total number of characters in the lexicon estimated at over 50,000, with a basic requirement to memorize 3,000–4,000 for literacy,[7] alongside the lack of a comprehensive phonetic framework of alphabet to navigate these, it is impossible to avoid the hard slog of rote memorization. This can play to the strengths of certain learners, who find this easier conceptually than trying to master complex grammatical systems with multiple declensions, conjugations, tenses and genders. A sense of achievement and gratification can be stronger with an easily quantified progress marker – how many characters do you know? However, it is hard to argue that this process of memorization in itself, if divorced from the cultural context and historical etymology, is particularly intellectually stimulating and therefore sustainable for more than a short-term intensive course. Add to this the fact that Chinese grammar is (particularly at the early stages) rather straightforward compared to many European languages, and that in modern Chinese most words are bisyllabic, and made up of two characters, thereby requiring students to learn all the combinations too, and learning Chinese can become a rather intensive, repetitive process.

Characters can be committed to memory in many different ways – some students find it easiest to analyse them into radical and phonetic, and make use of etymological insights, grounding them in traditional Chinese culture; others prefer to rely on the kinetic memory formed by frequent rewriting by hand; while others may prefer to compose their own stories based on the 'pictures' they see within them. In my experience of teaching Chinese to non-native speakers for over two decades, no single one of these methods works for all learners. Indeed one of the first tasks for students who are undertaking 'serious' study of Chinese is to discover which method works best for them.

On a very practical level, then, providing a cultural context for this learning can help alleviate the monotony of learning character after character. Traditional stories can sometimes shed light on why certain characters are used to form certain words. One famous example provides the origin of the Chinese word for 'contradiction', *maodun* 矛盾. The traditional story, originating from the writings attributed to the legalist philosopher Han Feizi 韩非子 (c. 280–233 BC), was of the stall owner selling spears and shields, who boasts that his spears (*mao*) were the sharpest in the world and could pierce anything and his shields (*dun*) were the strongest in the world and could withstand anything, and the quick-witted customer who asks what would happen if one of his spears were to attack one of his shields. I remember learning this story in my first year of studying Chinese and have never forgotten it. Not only does it teach us the etymological origin of the word, it also allows second language learners to connect with the traditional stories which Chinese school pupils would also learn, in the process of their language acquisition.

# As a way to develop cross-cultural understanding

As China's own attempts to 'go global' within the cultural sphere coincide with a heightened level of interest in the West in the deeper factors behind the country's much-vaunted economic rise, there is an obvious imperative to learn more of Chinese culture than just dragons, lanterns and lion dances. While it is really important to remember (and is often overlooked, especially in a classroom context) that culture is much more than simply literature, literary texts are a good place to start. I often tell my undergraduates that while they can read books and reports about Chinese society, economy and politics, and learn much about the nation in that way, by reading a novel, or other literary work, they are *experiencing* the culture, not as an 'other' but in much the same way as a Chinese person would engage with it. Without going into the nuances of postcolonial and orientalist discourses, on a very personal level, when a teenager in the UK reads a Chinese-authored YA book (whether in Chinese or in translation) this is a young person actually *participating in* a similar and non-hierarchical process of cultural acquisition to his or her counterpart in East Asia.

The response is not 'this is what Chinese people are like' but rather, 'this is how the Chinese book made me feel'.

Having said that, the increasingly global nature of Chinese literature today has been a topic of much academic debate over the last couple of decades – essentially whether or not contemporary Chinese writers are losing their 'Chineseness' and what this means. Research Window 1 provides an overview on some of these, often rather heated, discussions.

## Research Window 1: Chinese literature goes global

In 1990, in a controversial and highly influential essay, 'The anxiety of global influence: what is world poetry?', the eminent professor and translator Stephen Owen discussed what for him was the negative effect of globalization and cultural dominance of English language on contemporary Chinese poetry, where the translatability of language became a goal. In his words, 'They must write envisaging audiences who will read their work in translation' (Owen, 1990: 28–32). His focus is on poetry, but many of the statements he made could be equally applicable to other forms of literature. This has sparked off a vigorous debate, with Rey Chow (1993: 2) describing him as orientalist and even 'racist', believing that his problem is with the Western critic's loss of authority. She states, 'Owen's real complaint is that *he* is the victim of a monstrous world order in front of which a sulking impotence like his is the only claim to truth (3–4). In simple terms, the argument centres around whether or not Chinese writers adapt their writing to make it as 'translatable' and 'global' as possible, and in so doing diminish its literary quality, or whether in fact the people who are claiming this are simply guilty of essentializing and orientalizing by insisting that Chinese writers display their 'Chineseness'.

Other scholars also criticized Owen's approach and there is further discussion of both sides of the debate and its implications for the study of contemporary Chinese literature in the West in Andrew Jones (1994) and Maghiel van Crevel (2008), among others.

It is useful to bear these debates in mind when selecting and presenting texts to students, but equally if our basic approach is to one of cultural engagement and participation, then we can I think select texts primarily according to the engaging nature of their subject matter and the appropriateness of language level, while leaving the larger questions to the curriculum makers, policy makers and publishing houses.

To examine the process we undergo when we read the literature of another culture, let us turn back for a moment to the man credited with creating the very notion of 'World Literature'. As early as 1827, Goethe made his famous declaration that national literatures were losing their meaning, and 'the epoch of world literature is at hand'. Goethe's vision was based on national literatures coming together, in a term used by Julia Lovell among others, in a 'literary United Nations' (Lovell, 2006: 51).

Despite this, for the next century or so, the perception of world literature tended to imply anthologies of literature in English translation, with the usual criticism of Eurocentric bias and canon domination and so on. One of the foremost scholars today of world literature, David Damrosch, challenges this approach and, in his seminal study on the topic, he suggests that rather than a certain selection of works, what we should mean by world literature is a 'mode of circulation and of reading' (Damrosch, 2003: 5). He uses an anecdote about Goethe himself to further explore what this 'mode of reading' means.

> Dined with Goethe. 'Within the last few days, since I saw you', said he, 'I have read many things; especially a Chinese novel, which occupies me still and seems to me very remarkable.'
>
> 'Chinese novel!' said I; 'that must look strange enough.'
>
> 'Not so much as you might think', said Goethe; 'the Chinese think, act, and feel almost exactly like us; and we soon find that we are perfectly like them, except that all they do is more clear, pure, and decorous, than with us.'
>
> 'With them all is orderly, citizen-like, without great passion or poetic flight; and there is a strong resemblance to my *Hermann and Dorothea,* as well as to the English novels of Richardson.'
>
> (*Conversations with Goethe,* Johann Peter Eckermann (1835), cited in Damrosch [2003]: 10–11)

In his comments on the above exchange, Damrosch makes what is the most insightful and practical analysis of the processes and benefits of reading literature from another country that I have seen:

> Any full response to a foreign text is likely to operate along all three of these dimensions: a sharp *difference* we enjoy for its sheer novelty; a gratifying *similarity* that we find in the text or project onto it; and a middle range of what is *like-but-unlike* – the sort of relation most likely to make a productive change in our own perceptions and practices. (Damrosch, 2003: 11–12)

For me, Damrosch's critique of Goethe's conversation sums up neatly some of the most compelling reasons for both teachers and pupils to engage with foreign cultures through literature: first inspiration and enjoyment, then self-reflection and validation and ultimately greater cross-cultural understanding.

# Reading in the classroom

Despite these benefits, there are a number of practical obstacles to introducing Chinese literature into the classroom, which need to be addressed – the first of these are common to introducing any Chinese text, fiction or non-fiction.

# Preparing the text

While language teachers are doubtless familiar with the concept of pre-reading tasks, to get students to prepare their minds for reading, by providing context, vocabulary, etc., in advance, with Chinese I would suggest it is also useful to prepare the text itself.

First, presenting a long text in Chinese characters to non-native speakers is undeniably more intimidating than presenting a similar text in French or German. A key reason for this is the lack of phonetic clues – if you cannot read a text aloud or hear it in your head, it can be very disorienting.

Various attempts have been made in textbook formatting to overcome this. Some textbooks include the phonetic pinyin system (by which the Chinese city 上海 is transcribed to the familiar Shanghai). The immediate problem facing the typesetters is where to include the pinyin. If single sentences are provided, then the pinyin can usually fit underneath each character. With longer passages though, this can get messy. A paragraph of characters followed by a paragraph of pinyin provides few linkages for readers between the two ways of reading, and provides a strong disincentive for all but the most ardent lovers of Chinese script to focus on anything other than the Romanization. With the increasing use of online teaching materials, new possibilities are available, such as audio recordings to play next to the characters (thus negating the need for pinyin at all), so teachers should be mindful of making use of these developments.

Another problematic area is that of punctuation. In classical Chinese texts, there was often negligible punctuation of any kind, and most readers needed to rely on in-text commentaries for help breaking up the text to render it intelligible. While most Western forms of punctuation are used in Chinese texts today, there are still some stark differences, which can confuse and distract readers, and it is definitely worth considering providing students support with these, especially at pre-intermediate levels.

One issue is word spacing. In standard Chinese, individual Chinese characters are evenly spaced across the page. A full stop or comma takes up the same space as a character. Each character is a single syllable and has a discrete meaning, but the majority of words in modern-day Mandarin are made up of a combination of two characters. This can cause problems, as much time can be wasted looking up dictionaries only to discover that you have grouped the characters incorrectly, and that the first character you are looking for is in fact the final syllable of the previous word.

Some Chinese language textbooks aimed at non-native speakers, therefore they group characters in a word together, with a larger space between each combination. My only concern with this is that students do need to be prepared to encounter standard formatting and also ideally be aware of the whole spectrum of meanings that an individual character may have, to save time on the next encounter, in a different combination. I would suggest therefore a slight modification, namely that after they are familiar with a text, re-punctuated in this way, they are then asked to read through the same text but with standard spacing.

A second difference which regularly causes problems, often with hilarious results, is the fact that Chinese does not have an obvious way of distinguishing what in English are referred to as proper nouns. Names of people and places in Chinese are made up of meaningful characters, so 北 *bei* (north) and 京*jing* (capital) form Beijing, and so on. In general, Chinese names are two or three characters long. Names transliterated from Western languages can be much longer than this. A learner can waste lots of time pondering why the author has suddenly mentioned the 'bright moon' in the middle of a piece about an urban shopping mall, for example, before figuring out that '明月 *ming yue*' could simply be a reference to someone's boyfriend.

Again some textbooks choose to underline proper nouns and while this can help, if you do this in class then it is important that the lines do not interfere with the characters themselves, or this will cause even greater confusion. Highlighting proper nouns in colour or bold may be a more effective approach. It is also worth remembering that, while there are no hard and fast rules for this, identifying character strings which are likely to be names can be a very useful training for students. Rather than preparing this in advance, therefore, spending time in class looking at an unseen text and trying to pinpoint what combination(s) might be a name, and then highlighting these together with the students, along with repetitions of each string throughout the text, can also be a very fruitful pre-reading exercise.

## Extracting dialogue

At the risk of sounding like a broken record, we need always to bear in mind the disconnect between the spoken and written forms of Chinese. To put this another way, students need to constantly practise creating links between these two skills in order for their knowledge of the language to avoid becoming compartmentalized. Historically many eminent sinologists, and even translators, were famous for being unable to communicate in the spoken word at all. This was mainly due to the lack of access to China/Chinese people. The famous translator Arthur Waley, responsible for rendering a vast number of Chinese (and Japanese) works of poetry, fiction and philosophy into English, notably never visited East Asia and acquired his knowledge purely through long hours spent in the British Museum in London. Nowadays, it is highly unusual to find a Western student who can read Chinese fluently but struggles to communicate in the spoken language. There are still many cases though of students whose spoken Mandarin is competent but are functionally illiterate.

Assuming that as teachers we want our students to be employable in the twenty-first century and have competency in all four skills, we need to make more conscious effort to create linkages between them, in addition to linkages (as discussed below) with English. Using short extracts of dialogue from longer texts can work towards this, in various ways.

As a pre-reading task, after first describing the main protagonists in the proposed text, ask students to work in pairs to create imaginary spoken dialogues between two of the characters to help them predict vocabulary and content on a phonetic level. Then ask them to write these dialogues down to link the spoken and written forms and finally act out a role play in pairs.

When the characters in a plot are familiar to the reader, the text of the story itself becomes less daunting – often adjectives and descriptive phrases can be linked in the student's mind to one or other of the characters, thus helping facilitate vocabulary building.

Alternatively, if there is a dialogue within the text, then ask students to read this aloud first, with appropriate expression and discuss in English what the context and/or implications could be for such a conversation. This once again will provide a framework, both linguistic and conceptual, which equips students well to approach the main body of the text.

## Using technology

Electronic tools for reading Chinese have transformed the way second-language learners encounter the script. Just ten years ago, one of the main obstacles for engaging with a new article in Chinese language was the cumbersome nature of paper dictionaries. Since there is no clear way of knowing how to pronounce a previously unlearned character, even if your dictionary is arranged alphabetically, you had no easy way to search it. The search process involved a number of steps: identifying the radical (not always straightforward), finding the radical on a list in the dictionary index, counting the number of strokes of the rest of the character you are looking up and then searching through the list of characters with that number of strokes listed under the radical. This process would provide the pronunciation, which allowed you to look it up and find the meaning! Being given a short newspaper article as a student to prepare for the following week's class could involve several hours of slightly tedious dictionary work.

Nowadays the reading process can be very different. Freely available computer software (including simple add-ons to internet browsers) and electronic dictionaries provide instantaneous help with translating new characters and words. Mobile phone apps take this one stage further, with the ability to scan characters and get their meaning via OCR functions, and handwriting input methods to look for characters without needing to know the pronunciation. While the quality of computer translation as a whole has been much debated (and for Chinese, while it is improving rapidly, at time of writing there are still many problems), there is no question that this sudden explosion of electronic tools has revolutionized the learning process for Chinese second-language learners.

The net result of this is that accessibility to Chinese literature has been greatly enhanced and that authentic texts can now be used (with care) from a very early stage.

## Teaching Activity 1: Speed reading with electronic aids

Learning Objective: To overcome fear of confronting a text in non-Roman script by using familiar settings and electronic aids.

Choose a Chinese translation of a well-known fairy tale, for example, little Red Riding Hood 小红帽, but use any available.

- Ask pupils to use electronic dictionaries to try to decipher which story the translation is based on.
- Ask pupils to identify the name of the main protagonist(s) in Chinese and underline it each time it appears in the text.
- Ask pupils in pairs to compose a short dialogue in Chinese between the protagonists, and act it out.

Depending on classroom facilities, the story could be displayed on a website with, for example, the Google Chrome free add-on dictionary.

It can be adapted for various levels and ages of learner by modifying the choice of story, length of extract and/or by increasing the challenge of the post-reading language production task.

Electronic aids have had a huge impact. It is not all good news, however, I have noticed in recent years that my undergraduates who have used these tools to support their learning throughout their degree tend to struggle more with remembering word combinations, and with recalling the whole spectrum of a character's meaning, than those who persevered with paper dictionaries (or who could not afford a smartphone!). This is purely anecdotal, as I have not conducted a systematic study, but it is worth reminding students to avoid being overly reliant on technology – the tedious process of looking up a character manually may activate a longer form of memory than the instantaneous pop-up on Pleco.

# Translating across cultures

The relationship between translation and language teaching can be fraught. Translation Studies has quite rightly become an academic discipline in its own right, with vast numbers of articles and research monographs appearing every year analysing translation strategies and processes, from a broad range of perspectives, including both linguistic/textual analysis and sociological/cultural discourse. One of the drivers for the development of this thriving field is to confront the previous assumption that translation was just a mechanical process of switching vocabulary items from one language system into another and, by extension, nowadays the work of a professional translator can simply be replaced by using Google Translate.

Yet translation is regularly used within second-language classrooms, with little heed to these debates, as a means of assessment of student's comprehension of the source text. Teachers often assume that, if a student has English as a native (or near-native) language, then the process of rendering the foreign text they have been studying into that language is a straightforward one.

At a basic level, this is probably true. If we are teaching the question

银行在哪儿？(Yinhang zai nar?)

it is perfectly reasonable to ask the students to translate that into 'where is the bank?' A correct translation immediately indicates a grasp of both vocabulary and sentence structure (the Chinese word order is 'bank-is-where?').

When texts become more complex however, and particularly when literary texts are being used, the choices involved in rendering a text into English are far more numerous and nuanced. Chinese has no verb tense, no singular/plural, no conjugations of verbs or declensions of nouns and no definite/indefinite articles. As with all languages, there are many differences also in terms of vocabulary specificity, for example, Chinese extended families, where different members of the family all have specific titles (depending on whether they are your mother's elder brother or your father's younger brother, etc.), which would all usually get translated into the generic English terms for aunt/uncle and so on.

On a more theoretical level, there has been much debate about the extent to which translations should retain the 'flavour' of the original, as discussed in Research Window 3. While the vagaries of these debates are not directly relevant to the language classroom, they are of interest as discussion of the concepts of translation – the implications of different word choices, for example – can be a great way to provide follow-up activities for in-class practical translation tasks.

## Research Window 3: Foreignization or domestication in translation?

Lawrence Venuti in his 1995 classic *The Translator's Invisibility: A History of Translation* was the first to formally discuss the differences between domestication, 'bringing the author home' and foreignization, "sending the reader abroad" (1995: 20). He argues that the preference for fluency and domestication in translation has led to both the denigration of the status of the translator. If the ideal translator is invisible, as similar as possible to the author, and without his or her own voice or style, then this clearly implies a lack of agency or corresponding status.

Reflection point: When you read a translated novel, how conscious are you, or do you want to be, of the language of the original? Do you want to read it in the same way as you would read a novel written in your own language, or are you looking to be 'sent abroad'?

One practical instance of this, which is almost unavoidable in translating literature, is the thorny question of how to deal with names – do we transliterate them into pinyin or another Romanization form, convert them into English names, translate the meaning of the characters or a bit of mixture of all of these approaches?

Before we consider how to translate Chinese names, it is useful to reflect on what, if anything, we associate with names in English. Personally, I had always believed that the meaning of English names was irrelevant to English native speakers, until it came to choosing a name for my own children, at which point people gave me books with lists of names and definitions, and the task became rather stressful! Apart from in that very specific situation, however, it is debatable how often, if ever, the original meaning of say Sarah as 'princess' or Justin as 'righteous' really enter our consciousness in daily life. Other issues, such as background, age, class or gender, however, are sometimes inscribed in names, for native speakers at least.

Reflective task: To what extent in English do we think about the meaning of people's names, or do we just take them as signifiers (or ID tags) for the person? Imagine you going to a meeting, and you have been given a list of the names of the people who will be attending. Consider the list below (all common English names) – do you recognize any preconceptions you have about these names, and if so can you try to identify what these might be, in terms of gender/age/class/background etc.?

Andi, Boris, Christian, Delia, Edna, Francis, George, Henrietta, Isabella, Jimmy, Kylie, Leslie, Mary-Jane, Nelson, Oscar, Paddy, Rupert, Shane, Tracy, Ursula, Vikki, Xavier, Yolanda, Zane.

Different names may mean different things to different people – and you may genuinely have no expectation associated with most, or all, of these names.

> Bearing this in mind, consider the different approaches translators take to the translation of Chinese names. What impact do these have? Ask both Chinese native speakers and English native speakers if they have any association with the names of the protagonists in the stories you are reading.

Chinese names may reflect gender (but not usually as clearly as most English names do). They may reflect contemporary political concerns. They may indicate class or parental expectation. They may have a clear meaning associated with them, or a pun. They may have a classical allusion within them.

So, how to translate names can be a headache for translators. Some prefer never to translate the 'meaning' of the names, to avoid misleading English readers into believing that Chinese names are radically more semantically endowed than English ones.

Pinyin renditions of names may be easy for English native speakers to pronounce, for example, Wang Hongwen, or not, for example, Zhang Chunqiao. In a novel, if a name is hard for the reader to pronounce it is arguably hard to remember and possibly to relate to. Equally standard pinyin can cause other confusion for English readers, for example, 何小姐 Miss He or 舍先生 Mr She.

These issues are all potentially challenging for the would-be translator, but in terms of the language classroom, they again provide that much needed space for intellectual discussion *around* the language learning process, for reflection on the differences between the languages. These issues enrich the learning experience, help with the memorization of characters and allow the formation in the brain of those essential links between the two languages.

## What to read?

One of the main concerns raised by teachers facing the introduction of the new curriculum guidelines was that they did not know what texts to choose. Traditionally, Chinese fiction which was considered 'literary' was far from the colloquial everyday language spoken, and so to be truly 'literate' required considerable levels of education. The 'New Culture Movement' (also known as the May Fourth Movement) of the early twentieth century sought to address this and, along with the import of many Western literary theories and translated works, encouraged the publication of literature in the vernacular. The most well-known champion of this period, Lu Xun (1881–1936), is considered by many to be the 'father' of modern Chinese literature and his works quickly gained canonical status and many were included within Chinese curricula both within China and abroad. Indeed, moves in recent years to reduce the number of works by Lu Xun in Chinese secondary schools, apparently because they are 'too deep' and need to be replaced by more 'age-appropriate material', have been met with considerable controversy.[8] There is still today a reluctance to consider anything very contemporary as proper 'literature', and the latest writing is rarely included in curricula at Chinese universities, let alone at secondary schools.

By interpreting 'literature' broadly, there is a wide range of options for teachers when it comes to selecting material.

# Picture books

While you can debate for a long time about whether or not the nature of the Chinese script means there is something inherently more 'visual' about the Chinese language than roman scripts, there is no question that the relationship between Chinese characters, particularly (but not exclusively) calligraphy and pictures, is a close and complex one. Traditional painting more often than not has at least a few lines of calligraphy embedded within it, and the image would feel incomplete without the text. Modern-day picture books in China continue this tradition. They are hugely popular, and there is a strong interplay between the text and the image. While (as in the West) they are most frequently designed with very young children as their target readership, this is not always the case, and they can also be very useful in providing contextualization clues for readers. They are a ready-made resource for the 'predict the content' type of pre-reading task. They regularly deal with profound moral issues – and while the storyline may be rather didactic, by presenting it in simple language we can invite older students to discuss and challenge the moral as appropriate, perhaps in a post-reading speaking task.

Geoff Fox has previously advocated the use of picture books within the English literature curriculum at school. He notes, 'Picture books have been very helpfully used in the early weeks of literature courses for older students, since they raise certain issues about reading with particular clarity; the relationship between author and reader, how readers come to know what kind of a text they are handling, how readers need to move back and forth within a text, how endings are anticipated, for example' (1996: 600).

Sourcing suitable Chinese picture books in the West has become much simpler thanks to the efforts of publishers such as the US-based Candied Plums, whose bilingual versions of beautifully illustrated Chinese classics feature Chinese text with pinyin throughout, with a (good) English translation at the back of the book, along with some key vocabulary items.

---

## Teaching Activity 2: Picture books

The following activity is based on a workshop the Writing Chinese project conducted in London for over 100 secondary school students of Chinese. We used the picture book *The Peanut Fart* (2013) by Wang Xiaoming, trans. Adam Lanphier (Candied Plums, 2017), but alternative picture books could be substituted, preferably ones with a strong, and perhaps not too obvious, plotline.

Provide the title, the name of the main character and the illustrations, without the text. (The Candied Plums publications are particularly useful for this as they have thumbnail images at the back, without the text.)

Ask students to work in groups to predict the story.

Feedback to the whole class, and try to elicit the sort of vocabulary that might come up.

Then, if the students have electronic dictionaries, or are more advanced, ask them to work on the text in groups. For younger groups or for beginners, go through simple parts of the text as a whole class.

Provide the English translation of the whole text.

If appropriate, post-reading tasks could involve, for example, composing dialogues between characters, acting out the story or discussing what the target age group for the story would be.

# Poetry

The arguments for and against teaching Chinese poetry in the language curriculum encapsulate, for me, the different approaches to the use of literary sources.

The language of classical poetry is not easily transferable into modern conversation. For one thing, most of the syllables have a discrete meaning and are not arranged into bisyllabic combinations (the norm in modern standard Mandarin). The language is very concise and often intentionally ambiguous. Grammatical subjects are often omitted.

In 1987, Eliot Weinberger collated nineteen different translations of a single short Tang Dynasty poem by Wang Wei. With entertaining commentary from both himself and Octavio Paz, the variety of renditions contained within this small book, entitled *19 ways of Looking at Wang Wei*, provides an excellent introduction to the challenges and opportunities faced by would-be translators.

I have used this book in a course on literature in translation, in a mixed class made up of Chinese native speakers, Chinese second-language learners and literature students with no knowledge of Chinese. The Chinese poem was provided in Chinese script, pinyin Romanization (to allow all the students have some sense of how it might sound) and a literal English translation. I showed the students two or three of the published translations included in Weinberger's book and invited them to make their own.

It was a useful exercise for demonstrating the practicalities of the differences between the languages as well as providing a context for discussing the thorny issues of untranslatability – whether or not some poems or concepts simply could not be rendered from one language into another.

## Teaching Activity 3: Classical poetry

Choose a short classical poem (four-line *jueju* probably work best) and provide the pinyin plus either a literal English translation or for more advanced students ask them to provide one, using dictionaries/electronic aids as appropriate.

Ask the students to read the poem aloud (this can be a very focussed exercise where pronunciation problems can also be addressed if needed).

Discuss some of the typical features of the poem – for example, rhyme, line length, parallelism, etc. Discuss which, if any, of these could be translated into English.

Ask the students, in pairs, to provide an English version which works as a poem.

NB: There are many classical poems available in this format, with pinyin/literal translations already provided, both online and in, for example, Cai (2008) or Chang (2007).

# Literary texts in translation

Translated literature can provide an easily accessible background context to reading excerpts of literary works in the original language as well as being, in itself, an engaging window into broader cultural issues. But, as Research Window 4 demonstrates, English-speaking readers are still reluctant to read literature in translation, although the situation, particularly in the UK, does appear to be improving.

One frequent criticism of reading Chinese literature in English was that it could be bland or, in the worst-case scenario, unreadable. Certainly there have been great examples of wonderfully engaging translations (David Hawkes/John Minford's translation of 红楼梦 *Hong Lou Meng* as *The Story of the Stone* being a prominent example), but many more books were produced which could help Western readers understand what China was like, but were hard to engage with on an aesthetic level. Over the last decade or so, the quality of translated Chinese literature has improved vastly. We now have a broad selection of texts available, which work as literature.

## Research Window 4: Who reads literature in translation?

It is widely cited that translated literature (from any language) accounts for only 3 per cent of the English-reading book market. The 3 per cent figure is based on statistics in the United States and has been highlighted by the University of Rochester, which in 2007 developed an excellent Web resource on contemporary international fiction in translation and named the site after it (http://www.rochester.edu/College/translation/threepercent/index.php?s=about). In 2012, Dr Jasmine Donahaye produced a comprehensive report on the situation in the British Isles, which (while acknowledging some problems with data availability) suggests a slightly more optimistic picture, with between 4 per cent and 5 per cent of all literature being translations, and with a slight year-by-year increase. 'Three percent? Publishing data and statistics on translated literature in the United Kingdom and Ireland' are available at https://www.lit-across-frontiers.org/wp-content/uploads/2013/03/Publishing-Data-and-Statistics-on-Translated-Literature-in-the-United-Kingdom-and-Ireland-A-LAF-research-report-March-2013-final.pdf.

April 2016 marked the award of the hugely prestigious Hans Christian Andersen prize to Cao Wenxuan, the first Chinese recipient. Cao is a prolific writer of children's books, already a celebrity in China and now, with wonderfully moving translations by Helen Wang (the 2017 winner of the Marsh Award for children's literature in translation), is making something of a splash in the English-speaking world.

Partly to commemorate this award, in the summer of 2016 the Writing Chinese project held a symposium of roundtables in Leeds on children's literature, with translators, school teachers, librarians and academics. We gained an overview of the rich abundance of literature written for children in the world's largest nation and many fascinating insights into the agonies and ecstasies of rendering it into Western languages. For me, though, the highlight of the afternoon was a video recording from a bookclub set up at St Gregory's school in Bath, with two year 10 students giving very impressive reviews and observations of both Cao Wenxuan's *Bronze and Sunflower* and Shen Shixi's *Jackal and Wolf*, both of which were translated by Helen Wang. The school pupils had clearly enjoyed the books and compared the anthropomorphism insightfully to that of Western works they had read, discussed paratextual elements such as book covers and titles and generally provided a level of critical analysis which would put many undergraduate students to shame.

Above all, these reviewers proved that perhaps the new curricula, rather than simply being daunting and unrealistic, can, alongside the international recognition of Cao Wenxuan and the increased availability of English translations, provide a new opportunity to introduce young UK readers to the wonderful world of Chinese children's literature.

## In sum

The incorporation of literary texts into a language curriculum can add a layer of depth and colour to your classroom activity. Literature, whether in the original language or in translation, whether picture books or classical poetry, can provide a space for readers of any age to imagine, and engage with, another world. Reflecting on the process of translation allows us to reflect on ourselves. Yes, there are challenges, and texts should be selected and presented with care, but the rewards are certainly worthwhile.

### Useful online resources

*Chinese Books for Young Readers* (https://chinesebooksforyoungreaders.wordpress.com/) is a wonderful resource for children's literature from China, with an excellent blog and lots of bibliographical information.

The resources section of the *Modern Chinese Literature and Culture* site, hosted at Ohio State University (https://u.osu.edu/mclc/), has a fantastic collection covering both academic research on modern literature and lists of translations, author studies, etc.

*Paper Republic* (https://paper-republic.org/) is a collective of authors and translators of contemporary Chinese fiction. The site has a searchable database of free-to-view short stories.

*Writing Chinese* (https://writingchinese.leeds.ac.uk) has monthly bookclub with bilingual short stories, a book review network, translation competitions and schools bookclub.

## Notes

The introduction and context for this article are adapted from a blog post I originally wrote for the Chinese Books for Young Readers blog (https://chinesebooksforyoungreaders.wordpress.com/2016/09/14/chinese-childrens-literature-and-the-uk-national-curriculum/).

1. See, for example, 'How hard is it to learn Chinese?' http://news.bbc.co.uk/1/hi/magazine/4617646.stm (2006); 'Why native English speakers can learn Mandarin easily', https://www.britishcouncil.

org/voices-magazine/why-native-english-speakers-can-learn-mandarin-easily (2014); 'Learning Chinese is really, really hard, even for many Chinese people', http://www.latimes.com/world/asia/la-fg-china-mandarin-20160603-snap-story.html (2016). There are many similar articles and blogs available.

2. To read the full guidelines for the National Curriculum for Languages, including the breakdown for key stages 2 and 3, visit https://www.gov.uk/government/publications/national-curriculum-in-england-languages-progammes-of-study, published 11 September 2013.

3. https://www.gov.uk/government/uploads/system/uploads/attachment_data/file/485567/GCSE_subject_content_modern_foreign_langs.pdf.

4. https://www.gov.uk/government/uploads/system/uploads/attachment_data/file/485569/GCE_A_AS_level_subject_content_modern_foreign_langs.pdf.

5. Ibid.

6. https://ciforschools.wordpress.com/events/annual-chinese-teaching-conference/programme-2015/.

7. See, for example, http://asiasociety.org/china-learning-initiatives/chinese-writing.

8. See, for example, http://www.scmp.com/news/china/article/1305905/parents-angry-removal-luxuns-works-chinas-school-textbooks.

# References

Cai, Z. (Ed.). (2008). *How to Read Chinese Poetry*. New York: Columbia University Press.

Chang, E. C. (Ed.). (2007). *How to Read a Chinese Poem: A Bilingual Anthology of Tang Poetry*. South Carolina: Booksurge.

Chow, R. (1993). *Writing Diaspora*. Bloomington: Indiana University Press.

van Crevel, M. (2008). *Chinese Poetry in Times of Mind, Mayhem and Money*. Leiden: Brill.

Damrosch, D. (2003). *What Is World Literature?* Princeton, NJ: Princeton University Press.

Donahaye, J. (2012). 'Three Percent? Publishing Data and Statistics on Translated Literature in the United Kingdom and Ireland'. Available at https://www.lit-across-frontiers.org/wp-content/uploads/2013/03/Publishing-Data-and-Statistics-on-Translated-Literature-in-the-United-Kingdom-and-Ireland-A-LAF-research-report-March-2013-final.pdf.

Fox, G. (1996). 'Teaching Fiction and Poetry'. In P. Hunt (Ed.), *International Companion Encyclopedia of Children's Literature*. London; New York: Routledge.

Jones, A. E. (1994). 'Chinese Literature in the "World" Literary Economy'. *Modern Chinese Literature*, 8(1–2): 171–90. Also available at https://www.jstor.org/stable/41490729?seq=1#page_scan_tab_contents.

Lovell, J. (2006). *The Politics of Cultural Capital*. Honolulu: University of Hawaii Press.

Owen, S. (1990, November 19). 'The Anxiety of Global Influence: What Is World Poetry?' *The New Republic*, 28–32.

Venuti, L. (1995). 'The Translator's Invisibility: A History of Translation'. In E. Weinberger and O. Paz (Eds), *19 Ways of Looking at Wang Wei*. Rhode Island: Asphodel Press.

Wang, X. (2013). *The Peanut Fart*. Translated by Adam Lanphier. New York: Candied Plums.

# 6

# Teaching Poetry in Modern Foreign Languages

*Fotini Diamantidaki*

## Introduction

Recent changes in relation to the National Curriculum (NC) in England for modern foreign languages (MFL) teaching and learning have as its stated aim that to: 'Read literary texts in the language [such as stories, songs, poems and letters], (serves) to stimulate ideas, develop creative expression and expand understanding of the language and culture' (DfE, 2013: 1–2). Researchers (Collie & Slater, 1987; Hanauer, 2001, 2010) have discussed over the years the merits of teaching poetry in the foreign language classroom; Collie and Slater (1987: 226) pointed out successfully that 'poems offer a rich, varied repertoire and are a source of much enjoyment for teacher and learner alike'. They continued arguing that 'length' (226) is an obvious advantage for foreign language teachers and learners, as poetry may not be as daunting to read as a novel for example. More fundamental reasons are that poems explore 'themes of universal concern and embody life experiences, observations and the feelings evoked by them' (226). Poetry also offers strong imagery (226) and rhyming patterns that, if combined together, could possibly make a powerful pedagogic tool by bringing language into life. With this context in mind, the chapter proposes approaches to poetry that can be taught in MFL lessons, as a means to not only develop reading comprehension but also encourage students' engagement and personal interpretations.

## Initial approach to poetry

Hanauer (2010) presents the way he teaches poetry in his ESL college writing course through a series of workshops lasting eight weeks with the view of enhancing the creative expression of his students. This method of approaching poetry is constructivist as Hanauer (2010: 9) describes, where 'students choose their own sets of culturally specific poems (usually in their first language) to analyse for aspects of content and form. This method is accompanied by experimentation with poetry writing concerning their experiences'. Two elements are crucial here during the pedagogical technique: the choice of poems and students working in their first language. The choice of poems is left to the students and in their first language which facilitates the process of expressing their own experiences through poetry confidently. Even though this method is described as unfolding with adult ESL learners, I believe such approaches can also be successful with younger foreign language learners and offer an opportunity to work in collaboration across the English and foreign language departments in schools.

## Activity

Liaise with an English teacher in your department/school/institution, and discuss how they approach poetry. Make a list of the poems the students are studying in English, and aim to organize a creative writing session in collaboration with the English teacher where students can express their own feelings about their experience with the poem(s).

During Hanauer's workshops, once students engage with poetry in the foreign language, they are 'directed to the actual writing, reading, revision and presentation of their poetry' (2010: 9). What is fundamental during the revision of poetry is the emphasis on using language to accurately express the internal meanings and experiences of each writer. In other words, revision is directed 'not by language correctness in normative terms but rather through the consideration of accuracy of the expression to personally held understandings' (2010: 9). Therefore, the correctness in poetry writing is judged by how well the students expressed their own experiences with poetry and not how grammatically correct or incorrect the poem might be in the foreign language. The focus shifts to personal interpretation and responses to the poem, without focusing on grammatical accuracy, which can be a teacher's constant worry while students are producing a new piece of work.

## Activity

Initial engagement with poetry: Give your students a poem title in the foreign language you are teaching and choose two or three lines from the poem to accompany this. Using vocabulary they already know initially, ask them to express their opinions in the target language and their reactions. They could also write an alternative two lines or continue the two lines from the poem. Collect all the alternative lines or newly added lines of the poem from the class to create one poem.

This concept is based on the 'cadavre exquis' (exquisite corpse, literal translation), a collective writing game invented by the surrealists particularly Jacques Prevert and Yves Tanguy in 1925 in Paris. For more information on the game and its principles, please visit https://translate.google.co.uk/translate?hl=en&sl=fr&u=https://fr.wikipedia.org/wiki/Cadavre_exquis_(jeu)&prev=search.

Teachers eventually will correct the errors made, and Macaro, Graham and Woore (2016) highlight seven ways of giving feedback that he says are commonly found in research literature. Among the seven, the last three as presented by Macaro, Graham and Woore (2016) could be used to address students' grammatical errors:

'Reformulating: the teacher re-writes (a portion of) the students' work and gets her/him to compare the new version with the original. Editing instruction: the teacher gives instruction in editing strategies. Writing instruction: feedback is part of ongoing discussion during the writing process' (88).

In this way, the teacher encourages different personal interpretations without one right 'fits-all' answer. The teacher takes in consideration the different approaches in the class and, by encouraging multiple outcomes, recognizes that 'every pupil comes to the classroom with differences in experience and attitudes, ability and interests' (Holmes, 2002: 211).

All pupils have different experiences of the world outside the classroom (Holmes, 2002: 211) and it's an existing knowledge that goes unnoticed within the foreign languages classroom (Holmes, 2002: 211). Interpretative activities such as the one outlined above with poetry encourage personalized interpretations, 'unique to each individual' (Holmes, 2002: 211), that will 'enable students to build conceptual bridges between what goes on in their foreign language and real life' (Holmes, 2002: 211).

From personal experience, pupils often ask teachers why they have to learn a foreign language, as in their minds initially a 'foreign' language does not necessarily link to their reality. By building 'conceptual bridges' (Holmes, 2002: 211) via differentiated tasks and authentic stimuli, in our case poetry, not only can we bring the foreign language culture into the classroom but also offer the opportunity to make connections with pupils' own culture.

## Research window

Byram (1997) talks about the 'intercultural communicative competence': a process achievable by a number of *savoirs*. He defines the first savoir as the 'knowledge of social groups and their products and practices in one's own and in one's interlocutor's country, and of the general processes of societal and individual interaction' (Byram, 1997: 58). *Savoir-comprendre* is defined as 'the ability to interpret a document or event from another culture, to explain it and relate it to documents or events from one's own' (Byram, 1997: 61). *Savoir-apprendre/faire* is the 'skill of discovery and interaction: ability to acquire new knowledge of a culture and cultural practices and the ability to operate knowledge, attitudes and skills under the constraints of real-time communication and interaction' (Byram, 1997: 61). *Savoir s'engager* is 'the ability to evaluate, critically and on the basis of explicit criteria, perspectives, practices and products in one's own and other cultures and countries' (Byram, 1997: 63). Finally, *savoir-être* is 'the curiosity and openness, readiness to suspend disbelief about other cultures and belief about one's own' (Byram, 1997: 57).

To read the entire work please, follow the google books link: https://books.google.co.uk/books?id=0vfq8JJWhTsC&printsec=frontcover&dq=Byram,+M.,+(1997)+Teaching+and+assessing+intercultural+communicative+competence+Clevedon,+Multilingual+Matters.&hl=en&sa=X&ved=0ahUKEwiYu5PshI3bAhXkJMAKHVIcCNIQ6AEIJzAA#v=onepage&q=savoirs&f=false.

# Reading and topics

Drawing from my own experience within the classroom, reading in MFL lessons is an underdeveloped skill and considering that 'a lack of vocabulary knowledge is the largest obstacle for second-language readers to overcome' (Huckin & Bloch, 1993: 152), finding the 'effort of reading widely for general understanding is difficult and unrewarding. Such readers adopt a word-by-word processing approach which makes it very difficult for them to read for pleasure' (Ellis & Shintani, 2014: 172).

Bearing this in mind, introducing poetry in the language classroom can reinforce and develop reading skills with the view to eventually develop linguistic proficiency (Ellis & Shintani, 2014). Poems vary in terms of structure, length and complexity, and it can be argued that depending on the choice of poems teachers make to match the level of the students, it can make or break the lesson objective.

Examples of some every easy poems to include in a language lesson are interpretations of *Les Calligrammes* by Guillaume Apollinaire. He created poems according to different shapes and they can be viewed freely online (please see link in References section).

---

## Activity

Young learners can be encouraged to produce a version of a 'Calligramme', according to the topic vocabulary in any language they have been taught in class, or create a much longer version of a Calligramme with a combination of vocabulary and expressions.

---

This type of activity will encourage not only an artistic, more creative interpretation of vocabulary but it will also encourage them to memorize and retain it.

The activity above also suggests to integrate literature into topics. In schools, departments follow schemes of work based on a textbook or a thematic linear approach based on vocabulary groupings according to 'family, seasons, school, education, or items of clothing and indeed many more' (Diamantidaki, 2016: 58).

Relevant poems can be chosen by the teacher and integrated as one of the teaching resources used during the teaching of vocabulary and structures as a starting point. The table below illustrates the point made on the integration of poems within topics. The suggestion is to associate French poems and topics (thinking in terms of vocabulary and structure as presented in mainstreamed textbooks):

| Poems | Topics |
| --- | --- |
| 'J'aime ma mère' Maurice Carême | Family, structure 'I like' |
| 'Dans Paris' Paul Eluard | Prepositions, structure: il y a, places in town |
| 'L'écolier' Raymond Queneau | Travel and future tense |
| 'Déjeuner du matin' Jacques Prévert | Past tense |
| 'Demain, dès l'aube …' Victor Hugo | Future tense |

| Poems | Topics |
|---|---|
| 'Certitude' Paul Eluard | Conditional clauses |
| 'Dans les bois' Gérard de Nerval | Seasons, pronouns, negative |
| 'Le bonheur' Albert Samain | Family, adjectival agreements |

The rationale for such an association lies with the idea that if a poem 'is integrated into a topic it becomes more real, relevant to the curriculum and, most importantly, accessible to learners' (Diamantidaki, 2016: 59).

# Analysing the poem

The introduction of a poem by association with topics is only a starting point and a gradual, more in-depth approach would be the eventual aim. An approach that can allow students to access the poem, understand it and eventually interpret it, possibly reinvent it. To allow this to happen, a closer analysis of vocabulary followed by comprehension questions and possible interpretations is an idea.

As part of my PhD thesis (Diamantidaki, 2005), I developed a digital resource (CD-ROM) to suggest approaches to literary texts in foreign language lessons and among the genres studied were poems. The digital resource created was interactive and very similar to a website page, with the literary source and links to biography of the author on the main page of the poem. The two poems that I chose to illustrate here are 'le Pont Mirabeau' by Guillaume Apollinaire and 'Demain dès l'aube' by Victor Hugo.

Example 1: Le Pont Mirabeau, Guillaume Apollinaire

The snapshot illustrates how the poem looks on the resource with pedagogical features on the main page including links to vocabulary (words in purple): in the target language (synonyms) and in English, vocabulary is revealed when the pupil clicks and is directed onto a different page (an extract seen here as part of the figure). Three links also feature at the bottom of the page towards exercises at different levels for exploring the poem. The aim of having three different levels is for the gradual analysing of a poem that can move the learner from basic to in-depth comprehension, analysing the themes of the poem and suggesting some personal interpretations.

A resource such as the one above could be adapted for classroom use, without the use of digital resources. The concept behind it, where the teacher provides the poem, vocabulary with synonyms and/or translation and eventually tasks that allow a detailed analysis, could be organized in a similar way. The reason for integrating the poem at this level would be to attempt to go beyond the 'word-by word' (Ellis & Shintani, 2014) processing and observe initially how words function in context.

> ## Research window
>
> Chapter 7, from Ellis and Shintani (2014) on 'Teaching as an input', analyses pedagogical issues on authentic materials, teacher talk and extensive reading, among the analysis of four theoretical perspectives on input: the Incidental Learning Hypothesis, the Frequency Hypothesis, the Input Hypothesis and the Noticing Hypothesis. They are theories that can be associated with the approach undertaken here to analyse the poems.
>
> Limited preview of the book can be accessed online here: https://books.google.co.uk/books?id=mcs3AAAAQBAJ&source=gbs_book_other_versions.

# First reading

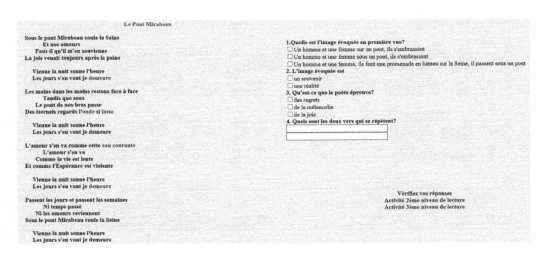

The first set of questions is based on observing the poem for its imagery and structure. The aim is for the pupil to grasp the basics: where the event takes place, what the event is/feeling of the poet is and noticing any repetition of verses and any structural specificity of the poem. The questions were crafted to illustrate how a teacher can guide the pupil to navigate the poem, encouraging a first reading, skimming and scanning and allowing pupils to develop gradual confidence with the text.

In practical terms, it would be a matter of creating multiple-choice questions (where/what) and highlighting any structural specificity, rather than requesting pupils to write in full sentences and in the target language. Key vocabulary for comprehension can also be accessed by clicking the purple words but vocabulary can also physically be provided alongside a poem in class. Alternatively, vocabulary could be taught during an earlier part of a lesson.

The resource as initially created above is an interactive one, with the possibility for pupils to check their answers (please see appendices), a feature that can encourage independent work. It is, however, just a suggestion and inevitably depends on each classroom teacher, context and how it feels best to conduct this type of activity.

## Second reading

1.Relevez les rimes du poème:

2. Qu'est- ce que vous observez?
☐ Elles sont constantes
☐ Elles ne sont pas constantes

3. Toujours au sujet des rimes:Qu'est-ce que vous observez entre le mot "peine" du premier vers et le mot "Seine" au dernier vers? Ainsi que entre "lasse" et "violente"?

4. Relevez les mots sur le sujet du temps et de l'heure

5. Par rapport aux mots relevés à quoi le temps est comparé?
☐ à l'eau qui coule
☐ à l'eau stagnante
☐ à la barque

6. Qu'est ce que le poète veut exprimer par rapport au sujet du temps?
☐ sa joie que le temps passe
☐ son regret que le temps passe
☐ l'amour qui s'enfuit au fil des années

Second reading encourages analysis of vocabulary, structures and themes in more detail. Many poems are stylistically rich in rhyme that could be judged worthy of carrying significance of meaning. Pupils are physically encouraged to type or write the rhymes of the poem, understand whether they are frequent or not and if they are repeated and how. They are then invited to type/write any words according to a reoccurring topic, in the case of 'Le pont Mirabeau', time. The analysis is gradually shifted towards metaphors, in the case of 'Le Pont Mirabeau', the metaphor between time and water and the significance that this may have for the poet.

A second reading invites the teacher to guide the pupils towards a stylistic discovery of the poem, either through rhymes, metaphors, repetition of words and noticing vocabulary according to themes. The teacher judges in advance what the poem has to offer from the above and organizes tasks accordingly. By engaging with the poem in such a way, it can allow students to make connections and start forming their own interpretations of the poem which in my view would be the ultimate aim during a third reading.

# Third reading

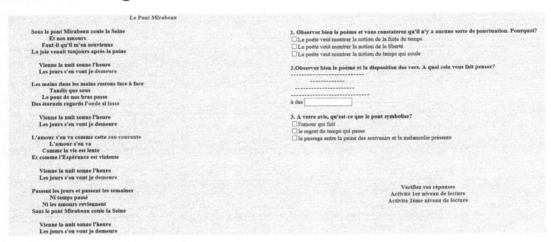

A third reading encourages further observations in the same line of thought as the second reading, working on stylistic specificities but advancing the thinking forwards into a more personalized interpretation. By observing the lack of punctuation in this poem, for example, the structure of the verses, the teacher can attempt to ask about the symbolism of the poem. Yet again, the teacher judges in advance which elements of the poem will be useful to highlight in order to guide the pupils towards their own interpretations. What is important to note is that no interpretation is wrong. Poetry offers polysemy of meaning and encourages personal interpretations and different reactions.

**Demain, dès l'aube...**
(le poème est adressé à la fille de V.Hugo, Léopoldine, qui est morte. Ca date de 1847 et c'est la veille de l'anniversaire de la mort de la fille).

Demain, dès l'aube, à l'heure où blanchit la campagne,
Je partirai. Vois-tu, je sais que tu m'attends.
J'irai par la forêt, j'irai par la montagne.
Je ne puis demeurer loin de toi plus longtemps.

Je marcherai les yeux fixés sur mes pensées,
Sans rien voir au dehors, sans entendre aucun bruit,
Seul, inconnu, le dos courbé, les mains croisées,
Triste, et le jour pour moi sera comme la nuit.

Je ne regarderai ni l'or du soir qui tombe,
Ni les voiles au loin descendant vers Harfleur,
Et quand j'arriverai, je mettrai sur ta tombe
Un bouquet de houx vert et de bruyère en fleur.

Vocabulaire

Activité 1er niveau de lecture
Activité 2ème niveau de lecture
Activité 3ème niveau de lecture

Victor Hugo: les contemplations, 1856
"Aujourd'hui", IV, XIV

Example 2: Demain dès l'aube, Victor Hugo

The layout is very similar to the previous poem, with links to the vocabulary and activities. A few more pieces of information on the context of the poem are given under the title and if explored pedagogically could help pupils understand the general mood of the poem. On the original page, there are also more links to other websites towards the authors' biography and other educational websites but they are not displayed here for copyright reasons.

# First reading

**1. Qui parle dans ce poème?**
☐ le père
☐ le poète
☐ le père - poète
**2. A qui s'adresse-t-il?**
☐ A une amante
☐ A une amante morte
☐ A sa fille
☐ A sa fille morte
**3. (1er vers): Dans quelle partie de la journée compte-il partir?**
☐ la nuit
☐ l'après-midi
☐ le soir
☐ l'aube
**4. (1er vers): Le père - poète nous met au courant de son trajet. Par où passera-t-il?**
☐ Il ira par la mer
☐ Il ira par la montagne
☐ Il ira par la campagne
☐ Il ira par la forêt

Vérifiez vos réponses
Activité 2ème niveau de lecture
Activité 3ème niveau de lecture

The multiple choice aims to explore four elements: who, to whom, when and where, presented in that order in the example. The above elements will not always be the same in every poem. Comparing both our examples here in this chapter, during the first reading, the basic elements of the poem previously deemed to be different (where/what) than the basics here (who, to whom, when, where). That means that as readers and teachers, there is a need to look at what type of information the individual poem offers in the first instance, elements that can allow pupils to grasp information based on questions such as who, when, what, where, when (not how and not why yet). Adding the location of the answer in the poem could be provided to the pupils, depending on whether teachers think the pupils need it or not. This differentiated feature will allow all pupils to access the poem.

## Second Reading

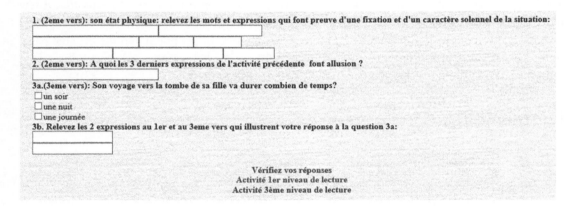

A second reading will build on the first reading by focusing on certain verses, words and expressions according to themes. The instructions are worded very carefully with indications of where the pupil can find the answers. The first question in this example focuses on typing/writing words and expressions that reveal the fixation of the poet and the obscurity of the situation. The second question attempts to make pupils think about why the poem has been written. The third question (both parts) focuses on the time of the day but also aims to reveal a metaphor. By wording instructions explicitly, it allows students even at word and expression level not only to access but also navigate the poem. Similarly to the first poem, in the second reading, teachers aim to locate words and expressions according to themes/metaphors and aim to move the questioning forward towards 'the why' and start observing the 'how'.

# Third reading

1.(3ème vers):quand il arrivera sur la tombe quelle sorte de fleurs mettra - t-il?

2.Qu'est-ce que la couleur verte et la fleur symbolisent à votre avis?
- ☐ la mort
- ☐ la vie
- ☐ la jeunesse
- ☐ la tristesse

3. A votre avis, suivant l'analyse pendant les 3 étapes, quelles sont les sentiments du père - poète?

Vérifiez vos réponses
Activité 1er niveau de lecture
Activité 2ème niveau de lecture

During a third reading, the pupil is guided towards a personal interpretation of the poem and questions encourage her or him to express own opinion. The process of the analysis moves to the how and why and the possible symbolisms the poem offers. More specifically in this example, the flowers that the poet is putting on the tomb are important here and what they symbolize, as are his feelings. So the pupils are guided through the questioning to make their own interpretations. If we observe the answers provided in the appendix of all the questions, from both examples, the reader will see that more than one answer is accepted during a third reading. This encourages multiple personal interpretations that poems can offer in abundance.

# Conclusion

There is still a lot of disagreement among L2 educators on the 'right' timing for introducing literature. These disagreements often depend on the educators' expectations (Carroli, 2008: 88), for example, if the teacher expects a perfectly accurate summary or literary analysis then it is likely that literature is introduced in the advanced classes (Carroli, 2008: 88). The key, in my opinion, is not only to choose the 'right' poem for the 'level' of the class and possibly the topic area the pupils are studying but also to allow access to the poem with clear linguistic tasks for their level. The source poem will not change; the approach that teachers can take needs to diversify according to each class.

In practise, this means a complete rethinking of the schemes of work and balance between using literature as a means to an end through 'a dynamic, student-centred approach' (Hişmanoğlu, 2005: 57) and pupils 'reading for pleasure' (Carroli, 2008: 94) so that the students develop their confidence. The approach suggested in this chapter aims to provide a solution towards that end and encourage personal involvement and interpretations.

From personal experience as an educator, and having tried this approach in schools with pupils for years, this approach to teaching literature helps develop a sense of achievement so that pupils move beyond the learning of decontextualized words and structures and a sense of accomplishment when they move to comprehension. When pupils sense that their own interpretations of the poems are correct, then something more beautiful occurs; not only they start loving the subject but also their confidence grows quickly in wanting to read more in the target language, for pleasure.

# Appendix

## A. Answers on first reading (Le Pont Mirabeau)

**1. Quelle est l'image évoquée en première vue?**
☐ Un homme et une femme sur un pont, ils s'embrassent
☐ Un homme et une femme sous un pont, ils s'embrassent
☑ Un homme et une femme, ils font une promenade en bateau sur la Seine, il passent sous un pont
**2. L'image évoquée est**
☑ un souvenir
☐ une réalité
**3. Qu'est-ce que le poète éprouve?**
☑ des regrets
☑ de la mélancolie
☐ de la joie
**4. Quels sont les deux vers qui se répètent?**
Vienne la nuit sonne l'heure
Les jours s'en vont je demeure

Retour activité
Activité 2ème niveau de lecture
Activité 3ème niveau de lecture

## B. Answers on second reading (Le Pont Mirabeau)

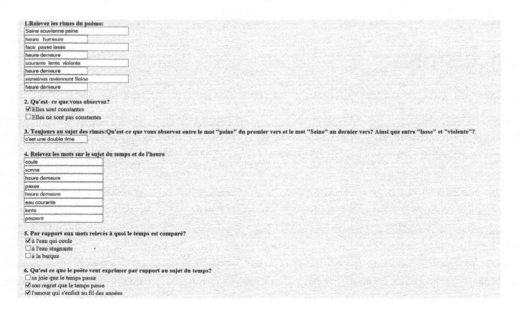

**1. Relevez les rimes du poème:**
Seine souvienne peine
heure humeure
face passe lasse
heure demeure
courante lente violente
heure demeure
semaines reviennent Seine
heure demeure

**2. Qu'est-ce que vous observez?**
☑ Elles sont constantes
☐ Elles ne sont pas constantes

**3. Toujours au sujet des rimes: Qu'est-ce que vous observez entre le mot "peine" du premier vers et le mot "Seine" au dernier vers? Ainsi que entre "lasse" et "violente"?**
c'est une double rime

**4. Relevez les mots sur le sujet du temps et de l'heure**
coule
sonne
heure demeure
passe
heure demeure
eau courante
lente
passent

**5. Par rapport aux mots relevés à quoi le temps est comparé?**
☑ à l'eau qui coule
☐ à l'eau stagnante
☐ à la barque

**6. Qu'est ce que le poète veut exprimer par rapport au sujet du temps?**
☐ sa joie que le temps passe
☑ son regret que le temps passe
☑ l'amour qui s'enfuit au fil des années

# C. Answers on third reading (Le Pont Mirabeau)

**1. Observez bien le poème et vous constaterez qu'il n'y a aucune sorte de ponctuation. Pourquoi?**

☑ Le poète veut montrer la notion de la fuite du temps

☐ Le poète veut montrer la notion de la liberté

☑ Le poète veut montrer la notion du temps qui coule

**2. Observez bien le poème et la disposition des vers. A quoi cela vous fait penser?**

----------------------------

--------------

----------------------

----------------------------------

à des | vagues / ondes |

**3. A votre avis, qu'est-ce que le pont symbolise?**

☑ l'amour qui fuit

☑ le regret du temps qui passe

☑ le passage entre la peine des souvenirs et la mélancolie présente

# D. Answers on the first reading (Demain dès l'aube)

**1. Qui parle dans ce poème?**

☐ le père

☐ le poète

☑ le père - poète

**2. A qui s'adresse-t-il?**

☐ A une amante

☐ A une amante morte

☐ A sa fille

☑ A sa fille morte

**3. (1er vers): Dans quelle partie de la journée compte-il partir?**

☐ la nuit

☐ l'après-midi

☐ le soir

☑ l'aube

**4. (1er vers): Le père - poète nous met au courant de son trajet. Par où passera-t-il?**

☐ Il ira par la mer

☑ Il ira par la montagne

☐ Il ira par la campagne

☑ Il ira par la forêt

Retour activité
Activité 2ème niveau de lecture
Activité 3ème niveau de lecture

# E. Answers on the second reading (Demain dès l'aube)

**1. (2ème vers): son état physique: relevez les mots et expressions qui font preuve d'une fixation et d'un caractère solennel de la situation:**

| | | |
|---|---|---|
| Je marcherai les yeux fixés sur mes pens | Sans rien voir au dehors | |
| sans entendre aucun bruit | Seul | inconnu |
| le dos courbé | les mains croisées | Triste |

**2. (2eme vers): Qu'est-ce que les 3 derniers expressions de l'activité précédente font allusion à votre avis?**

un pelerinage

**3a.(3ème vers): Son voyage vers la tombe de sa fille va durer combien de temps?**

☐ un soir
☐ une nuit
☑ une journée

**3b. Relevez les 2 expressions au 1er et au 3eme vers qui illustrent votre réponse de l'activité 3a:**

dès l'aube
or du soir

Retour activité<br>
Activité 1er niveau de lecture<br>
Activité 3ème niveau de lecture

# F. Answers on the third reading (Demain dès l'aube)

**1.(3ème vers):quand il arrivera sur la tombe quelle sorte de fleurs mettra - t-il?**

houx
bruyère en fleur

**2.Qu'est-ce que la couleur verte et la fleur symbolisent à votre avis?**

☐ la mort
☑ la vie
☑ la jeunesse
☐ la tristesse

**3. A votre avis, suivant l'analyse pendant les 3 étapes, quelles sont les sentiments du père - poëte?**

par rapport a votre sensibilite....

Retour activité<br>
Activité 1er niveau de lecture<br>
Activité 2ème niveau de lecture

# References

Byram, M. (1997). *Teaching and Assessing Intercultural Communicative Competence*. Clevedon: Multilingual Matters.

Carroli, P. (2008). *Literature in Second Language Education: Enhancing the Role of Texts in Learning*, 6–18. London: Continuum.

Collie, J. and S. Slater (1987). *Literature in the Language Classroom: A Resource Book of Ideas and Activities*. New York: Cambridge Universities press.

DfE. (2013). 'Languages Programmes of Study: KS3'. Online. Accessed 9 July 2018 from www.gov. uk/government/uploads/system/uploads/attachment_data/file/239083/SECONDARY_national_ curriculum_-_Languages.pdf.

Diamantidaki, F. (2005). *Internet et Documents Littéraires: Un moyen d'enseigner la langue, Nice Sophia Antipolis*. PhD thesis.

Diamantidaki, F. (2016). 'Using Literature in the KS3 Foreign Language Classroom'. In C. Christie (Ed.), *Success Stories from Secondary Foreign Languages Classrooms: Models from London School Partnerships with Universities*. London: Trentham.

Ellis, R. and N. Shintani. (2014). *Exploring Language Pedagogy through Second Language Acquisition Research*. New York; London: Routledge.

Hanauer, D. (2001). 'The Task of Poetry Reading and Second Language Learning'. *Applied Linguistics*, 22(3): 295–323. https://doi.org/10.1093/applin/22.3.295.

Hanauer, D. (2010). *Poetry as Research: Exploring Second Language Poetry Writing*. Amsterdam: John Benjamins.

Hişmanoğlu, M. (2005). 'Teaching English Through Literature'. *Journal of Language and Linguistic Studies*, 1(1): 53–66.

Holmes, B. (2002). 'Differentiation'. In S. Ann (Ed.), *Aspects of Teaching Secondary Modern Foreign Languages Perspectives on Practice*, 211–21. London: Routledge.

Huckin, T.. and J. Bloch. (1993). 'Strategies for Inferring Word Meaning in Context: A Cognitive Model'. In T. Huckin, M. Haynes and J. Coady (Eds), *Second Language Reading and Vocabulary Learning*, 153–76. Norwood, NJ: Ablex.

Macaro, E., S. Graham and R. Woore. (2016). *Improving Foreign Language Teaching: Towards a Research-Based Curriculum and Pedagogy*. Oxon and New York: Routledge.

## Poem links

Apollinaire, G. (1918). Les Calligrammes, https://publicdomainreview.org/collections/apollinaires-calligrammes-1918/, accessed 24 May 2018.

Apollinaire, G. (1913). Le Pont Mirabeau, recueil de poèmes Alcools, http://www.toutelapoesie.com/poemes/apollinaire/le_pont_mirabeau.htm, accessed 24 May 2018.

Carême, M. (1935). J'aime ma mère, recueil de poèmes: ma mère, http://maurice-careme-ses-poesies.blogspot.co.uk/2012/01/jaime-ma-mere.html, accessed 23 May 2018.

Eluard, P. (1951). Certitude, Recueil de Poèmes: Le Phénix, http://www.unjourunpoeme.fr/poeme/certitude, accessed 24 May 2018.

Eluard, P. (1989). Dans Paris, Recueil de Poèmes: Poésie intentionnelle et poésie involontaire, http://www.paris-a-nu.fr/paris-poesie-dans-paris-de-paul-eluard/, accessed 24 May 2018.

Hugo, V. (1847). Demain dès l'aube, Recueil de Poèmes: les Contemplations, https://www.poetica.fr/poeme-63/victor-hugo-demain-des-l-aube/, accessed 23 May 2018.

Nerval, D. G. (1853). Dans les bois, Recueil de Poèmes: Odelettes, http://www.poesie-francaise.fr/gerard-de-nerval/poeme-dans-les-bois.php, accessed 23 May 2018.

Prévert, J. (1947). Déjeuner du matin, Recueil de Poèmes: Paroles, http://www.rhs-giessen.de/data/comenius/gedichtband/data/FR/uebersetzung.pdf, accessed 23 May 2018.

Queneau, R. (1968). L'écolier, recueil de Poèmes: Battre la campagne, https://www.poetica.fr/poeme-844/raymond-queneau-ecolier/, accessed 23 May 2018.

Samain, A. (1898). Le Bonheur, Recueil de Poèmes: Aux flancs du Vase, http://www.poesie-francaise.fr/albert-samain/poeme-le-bonheur.php, accessed 23 May 2018.

# 7

# Literature and the Target Language

*Colin Christie*

## Introduction

This chapter will examine ways of exploring literary texts through the medium of the target language. While teachers may be convinced of the value of studying a literary text, they may be less confident about doing so in the target language itself. This might be due to a concern that their learners will not understand and/or do not have the necessary language to engage with texts in a meaningful way. Furthermore, it could be felt that time constraints and the pressures of examinations do not allow for work on texts to be undertaken in the target language. Here we will look at ways of giving learners the target language tools needed to talk about literary texts by identifying and teaching them the exact language they need. It is argued that this language is equally valuable for use in other contexts. Interesting and interactive ways of giving learners this input and helping them to practise it will be shared. Second, ways of motivating learners to use this target language to talk about the texts will be considered.

## Literature for all

The study of literature in a foreign language in the UK has traditionally been reserved for higher levels of study, for example at A level or at university. More recently, however, it has been included in the National Curriculum (DfE, 2013), opening it up to younger learners. This has resulted in secondary school pupils at key stage 3 (aged 11–14 years) reading and understanding literature in a foreign language. This focus can continue into key stage 4 as literary extracts are now included in the General Certificate of Secondary Education (GCSE) reading examination (AQA, 2016a). At A level, it has been possible to study a literary text and write about it in the target language as a piece of coursework. The new A level, however, makes the study of at least one literary text and a target language essay on the text a compulsory part of the specification (AQA, 2016b). In the French specification, for example, one of the texts is Albert Camus' *L'Étranger* (1988) and learners prepare to write an essay in the final examination. What makes this particularly demanding is that the essay has to be written under examination conditions in response to an unknown question.

For the 2016 (for 2018 examination) specimen papers, these questions are as follows:

1   Analysez comment le comportement et les attitudes de Meursault mènent à sa mort à la fin du récit.
2   Dans quelle mesure peut-on dire que L'étranger est un récit philosophique?

(AQA, 2016b)

1   Analyse how the behaviour and attitudes of Meursault lead to his death at the end of the story.
2   To what extent can we say that L'étranger is a philosophical story?

It is clear that teachers at different key stages may want to approach literature in different ways. Those preparing learners for the GCSE examination may want to focus on the comprehension of short literary texts and the answering of exam-style questions on them. Those working with A level learners may focus much less on using the target language to demonstrate understanding of the text but emphasize written production, discussing and analysing the text concerned.

Teachers of key stage 3 classes may expose their learners to short pieces of literature, for example, poems or songs, but not necessarily ask learners to show understanding of them or write about them in the target language. They may be happy to include such cultural elements in their lessons but not see the need to use the target language to explore them.

Coffey (2016) points out how there has long been a traditional separation between language and literature, the former being skill-focused and the latter content-focused. He describes this separation as something of a false dichotomy, claiming as follows:

> The nuts and bolts of language work (grammar, lexis, syntax) can be achieved through the exploitation of literary texts just as much as through newspaper articles or sound recordings of interactional language. (2016: 80)

It is argued here that literary texts are a perfect context for language study, being rooted in the target language culture as they include authentic content which stimulates learners. In this way, Coffey's 'language-as-a-skill' and 'literature-as-content' (2016: 80) can be effectively combined.

The question of the extent to which the target language should be used in class is a long-running one. One could put forward a number of reasons why literature should be examined in the L1. It might, for example, be more efficient, ensure the text is fully understood and also make sure that the study of literature is not devoted time which might otherwise be used to cover the various topics of the scheme of work or the GCSE specification. Use of the target language to explore literary texts, however, can allow learners to reinforce and expand their use of the target language, as in doing so they can encounter and use much language which is also useful for examination purposes. This can include the language of description, opinions and different tense forms, all important in the GCSE examination.

My own research into the promotion of spontaneous target language talk in the modern foreign languages classroom identified two key areas which need to be present and to be managed (Christie, 2017): target language management and context management. In terms of management of the target language, first the actual language needed by learners has to be identified and taught explicitly. Certainly in the initial stages of learning, and indeed beyond, chunks and formulas provide a useful framework for the provision of this language. Second, this language needs embedding into the learners' repertoire of language through systematic practice. If this stage is omitted, then learners may well lack the confidence and knowledge to communicate in the target language and revert to English instead. Further, not only the target language but also the context needs managing so that learners are incentivized to speak the target language. The findings of my study that the expression of emotions, the use of reward and the use of competition promote target language use can also be transferred to the context of literature as will be explored later on. We shall first of all examine the aspects of target language management.

# Teaching the language: giving learners the tools for target language talk about literature

A fundamental requirement for the promotion of target language talk about literature is the need to identify the language needed and to teach it explicitly. This may appear an obvious point but it is often overlooked. Learners are provided with the language necessary to understand the text but not that needed to talk about it. Both Macaro (2000) and Crichton (2009) acknowledge that where more spontaneous pupil talk does take place it is only due to the fact that it has been taught by the teacher in the same way as topic language is taught and that pupils gained from the teacher the vocabulary and structures they needed (Crichton, 2009).

One common barrier to the use of the target language by students to talk about any topic, then, including literature, is that they simply have not been taught the language they need. Even if they have been taught the language, it has often not been rehearsed and practised enough for learners to want to use it spontaneously and confidently to talk about literature.

The key here, as with language for any other purpose, is for the teacher to plan meticulously the exact vocabulary, structures and phrases he or she wants the learners to produce and then to plan the teaching of these. Ideally, learners would then have the opportunity to practise it, as they would any other language, before using it in the context of talking about literature.

The starting point for the teacher aiming to promote the target language teaching of literature is to identify specific phrases that learners will need so that they can easily reuse them in the form taught (Christie, 2017: 80). Many of these will be in the form of chunks which learners can reapply. Ellis (2008: 431–2) notes how learners need to 'acquire a solid repertoire of formulaic chunks'. Arnold, Dornyei and Pugliese (2015: 10) talk about the 'formulaic language principle', one of their seven main principles of the Principled Communicative Approach (PCA). They note how items of language should be selected and 'practised and recycled intensely' (2015: 10).

In the realm of literature and indeed culture in general, one may well study a cultural artefact or extract of literature in the target language, but any discussion around its context or origins may well be in English, for the sake of saving time or ensuring comprehension. While my own study focused primarily on the spoken production of language rather than reading comprehension, the above principles can first be transferred to helping learners understand the context of a literary text, as we will now explore.

## Chunks for comprehension

The following example, which introduces the author Rafael Alberti, author of the Spanish poem 'La Paloma' uses a number of techniques for making the target language explicit and accessible. The teacher has identified key words – or chunks – and these are provided in English. Furthermore, they are transferable words or chunks that can be applied to other authors, allowing learners to build up a repertoire of language with which to talk about any author. Learners then use this to help them put the English summary sentences in the correct order.

---

**PISTAS: Fue**: He was **Nació**: He was born **Falleció**: He died **Ganó**: he won **Marcó un hito**: it was a key moment **Escribió**: He wrote **Conoció**: He met **Durante**: during **expresó su postura**: he spoke out (politically) **Vivió en el exilio**: he lived in exile **desde … hasta**: from … to . . .

*Rafael Alberti*

Rafael Alberti **fue** un importante escritor español. Fue autor de una extensa lista de poemas y **ganó** el Premio Nacional de Poesia. **Nació** en Cádiz en 1902 y **falleció** en la misma ciudad en 1999. La muerte de su padre en 1920 **marcó un hito** en la vida de Rafael: fue ése el momento en que **escribió** sus primeros versos. **Conoció** a Federico García Lorca entre otros brillantes jóvenes. Durante la Guerra Civil **expresó su postura** Antifascista. Más tarde, **vivió en el exilio** en varias partes del mundo, **desde** París **hasta** Buenos Aires.

| 1 | 2 | 3 | 4 | 5 | 6 | 7 | 8 |
|---|---|---|---|---|---|---|---|

*Rafael Albertí; Pon las frases en el orden correcto según el texto:*

   **A.** He was born in Cadíz in 1902.
   **B.** In exile, he lived in France and Argentina.
   **C.** The death of his father was very significant in his life and inspired him to start writing poetry.
   **D.** He died in the same town he was born in 1999.
   **E.** He was an important writer of poetry.
   **F.** He wrote an extensive list of poetry, and he won the National Poetry Prize.
   **G.** He was an anti-fascist during the Civil War.
   **H.** When he was young, he was friends with Lorca (the most famous Spanish writer).

---

The examples below also illustrate how the teacher has simplified language to provide information about an author and make this information accessible to the learner in the target language:

> **Le Petit Nicolas**
> Le Petit Nicolas *est* un livre.
> *Il a été écrit par* René Goscinny *et illustré par* Jean-Jacques Sempé.
>    Le livre *est sorti en* 1959. Le film *est sorti en* 2009.

The phrases in italics are chunks of language which can be learnt and drilled (the importance of the drilling of language will be discussed in a later section). They can then be reused for other items of literature or indeed for films. The above example was used with a Year 7 class and it may be argued that the use of the passive voice in some of these chunks is too advanced for this stage. However, it is perfectly acceptable to use some language as a chunk without explicitly expecting learners to be able to manipulate it, so long as its meaning is understood. Indeed, some learners may well go onto to be able to manipulate or form this structure, if even by simply substituting words. Others might be content just to reproduce them as they stand.

Comprehension of events can also occur by using simplified, concise target language. Below are some summary sentences about Le Petit Nicolas which learners can put in order, or link to images:

> *Le lieu*
>
>    Avant l'école
>    A l'école- dans la salle de classe
>    A l'école- dans la cour de recreation
>    En rentrant à la maison
>    Chez un copain
>    Dans le parc
>
> *Les événements*
>
>    Un nouveau garcon est arrivé
>    Un nouveau professeur est arrivé
>    On a fait un voyage scolaire
>    C'est le premier jour de l'année scolaire
>    Ils font une potion magique

The following target language description of French poet Robert Desnos is also an example of simplified text. The use of cognates or near cognates has been highlighted in italics and makes the text accessible:

> Robert Desnos *était* un *poète* français. Il est né en 1900 à Paris. Ce poéte s'est *interessé au surréalisme*. Cet homme était un *génie du poème*. Desnos était aussi très *attiré par le cinéma et par la radio*. Il est mort en 1945 dans un *camp de concentration* en République Tchèque quelques mois avant la fin de la guerre.

Another area where target language use can drop out is in the comprehension of the text itself. It is sometimes a challenge to work one's way through a text and ensure a class has understood it. The following activity offers an interactive student-led way of understanding a text while at the same time involving confident target language production. Learners need to be taught and drilled the following phrases in the target language:

> How do you say … in English?
> You say …
> In the Spanish example below, this is:
> ¿Cómo se dice … en inglés?
> Se dice … en inglés

In my research, I called this a 'target language lifebelt' (Christie, 2017: 81), a phrase useful for learners in any context. It allows them to ask for language at any point and helps overcome the issue of the learners' being a passive recipient of language which he or she may not understand. It allows the learner to play an active part in the comprehension process.

In this activity, then (called 'Quiz, Quiz, Trade'), learners are given a word from the text and have to go round the class asking a partner, in the target language, the meaning of their word in English. Their partner does the same with them. On completion of the task, the two learners swap papers and then continue around the room, asking the meaning of their new word. This carries on until the end of the activity. This is an interactive and interesting way of helping learners cover the meaning of the vocabulary of the poem:

---

¿Cómo se dice **el trigo** en inglés?
Se dice **wheat** en inglés

¿Cómo se dice **el agua** en inglés?
Se dice **water** en inglés

¿Cómo se dice **el mar** en inglés?
Se dice **the sea** en inglés

¿Cómo se dice **la noche** en inglés?
Se dice **the night** en inglés

¿Cómo se dice **la mañana** en inglés?
Se dice **the morning** en inglés

¿Cómo se dicen **las estrellas** en inglés?
Se dicen **the stars** en inglés

¿Cómo se dice **la rocio** en inglés?
Se dice the **dew** en inglés

¿Cómo se dice **la calor** en inglés?
Se dice **heat** en inglés

¿Cómo se dice **el trigo** en inglés?
Se dice **snowfall** en inglés

¿Cómo se dice **creyó que** en inglés?
Se dice **she/he thought that** en inglés

¿Cómo se dice **la blusa** en inglés?
Se dice **blouse** en inglés

¿Cómo se dice **el cielo** en inglés?
Se dice **the sky** en inglés

¿Cómo se dice **tu corazón** en inglés?
Se dice **your heart** en inglés

¿Cómo se dice **la orilla** en inglés?
Se dice **the shore** en inglés

¿Cómo se dice **una rama** en inglés?
Se dice **a branch** en inglés

A further activity which can consolidate comprehension is examining a text for synonyms and antonyms. Not only does this allow spoken discussion but it also helps learners engage cognitively with language as it is a challenge to identify words of similar and opposite meaning. The word 'antonym' itself is a useful concept and has links with literacy in English.

The example below is from the Spanish poem 'La Paloma'. One particular advantage of this poem is that it contains a number of antonyms and the teacher here has identified this as a helpful starting point for the lesson.

Learners engage in a target language dialogue as follows:

**Persona A:** ¿Qué es un antónimo para 'limpio'?
**Persona B:** Creo que es 'sucio'
**Persona A:** Estoy de acuerdo
**Persona A:** ¿Qué es un antónimo para 'feo'?
**Persona B:** Creo que es 'moderno'
**Persona A:** No estoy de acuerdo. Creo que es 'bonito'

| | | | |
|---|---|---|---|
| **1** | limpio | A. | pequeño |
| **2** | feo | B. | padre |
| **3** | antiguo | C. | sucio |
| **4** | grande | D. | moderno |
| **5** | madre | E. | calor |
| **6** | frío | F. | bonito |
| **7** | norte | G. | sur |

There are, of course, other ways in which learners can work on the comprehension of a text through engaging with activities in the target language. These are activities which one can easily adapt from reading comprehension approaches to other topics. Some examples for a poem are shown below:

## Non-verbal responses: Circling or underlining words

Dans chaque vers, la scène où se passe-t-elle? Encerclez le bon mot dans chaque vers.
Soulignez les verbes en rouge, les adjectifs en vert et les noms en bleu.

Where does the scene take place in each line? Circle the correct word in each line.
Underline the verbs in red, the adjectives in green and the nouns in blue.

## Finding equivalents

Trouvez le français/ Trouvez l'anglais

At key stage 5, use of the target language for the study of literature is much less controversial. As Pachler and Allford (2000: 244), having discussed a range of reasons for studying literature, point out,

> It is worth mentioning that at A-Level and beyond, all the activities implied under the above headings could be carried out largely or exclusively in the TL.

An issue which arises at key stage 5 is that the teacher will often want learners to read a section of text for themselves in advance of the lesson. This will enable more interesting work to be done on the text itself during the lesson, without having to cover the basic comprehension of the text. Nevertheless, there is the dilemma of the extent to which one can assume that the homework reading has been done and/or that the text has been understood correctly. As a result, it is important to check the comprehension each time but without doing this in a tedious way which simply replicates the reading of the text together. Below are suggestions for activities in the target language which can help with this process.

## Questions in the target language with reference to pages/paragraphs

One can set questions in the same way that one would for any text. These not only test comprehension but also provide a useful summary to which students can refer. If one has set several pages to be read for homework, indicate which page number the question refers to in order to enable students to access this or quickly. Question types can be ones which commonly feature for other reading texts, for example,

- True/false
- Match sentence beginnings and endings
- Multiple choice: Choose the correct statement from a choice of two or three statements

# Put events in the correct order

This is a straightforward exercise but again a very useful one. It enables students to have a very clear summary and sequence of events in the book or play and it also ensures that work is done in the target language. At the same time, this sort of work on literature is not a separate part of language learning, as reading comprehension skills are being reinforced and possibly new language introduced.

# Questions in the target language with reference to characters

Questions which relate solely to the chronology of the text, as the action/ plot evolves, become tedious after a while. It is, therefore, helpful to vary this approach a little by having questions which relate to individual characters. In the same way that general questions can provide students with a summary of the text, questions on characters enable students to build up a picture of relevant events in the book which cast light on character development.

# Quotes: Who? Context. Analysis

Another variation on work around characters is to provide quotes from the dialogue. Students then have to identify who is speaking. This is still working very much at the level of comprehension but it is a different approach and again one which reinforces the importance of understanding the individual characters. In terms of differentiation, this can be taken further by giving quotes that have words missing in them (a gapped text). This not only increases challenge but is also a useful language learning activity in itself. Of course, the missing words can be provided in a separate box if this support is required.

# List of key points in text for each character

As they go along with their reading, students should be encouraged to keep a list of key points and quotes in the life of each character.

# Grammatical exercises and translation

Of course, there is nothing to stop the teacher using extracts from the literary text as they would any other piece of language to advance grammatical knowledge through grammatical activities.

## Chunks for production of opinions about characters and events

The examples above focused primarily on the understanding of the target language, although of course there is no reason why these chunks cannot then be reused in spoken or written production of the language. The examples below target mainly the production of language and provide the tools for learners to talk about literature in the target language.

The following language is intended for use when learners are speculating upon what characters in the text might be like. This may be from a visual stimulus, such as a book cover or a quote or extract:

| A mon avis, | il | va | être | cruel/gentil |
| | elle | va | être | cruelle/gentille |

This language incorporates the giving of opinions crucial for the GCSE examination and also reinforces the future tense. This point underlines how discussion of literature in the target language can support language learning generally across all topics.

Chunks are sometimes seen as being restrictive as they do not allow the learner to create meaning for themselves. I have argued that this is not the case as they can form the basis of more creative utterances. Myles, Mitchell and Hooper (1999) note how formulas and chunks are the *starting point* for creative construction in the language. I have shown (Christie, 2017: 82) how chunks can develop and that they operate at three levels. Level one involves the learner simply replicating the chunk as taught by the teacher, in its original form. In the context of literature, this might be as follows:

A mon avis le poème est très amusant

Level two involves the learner building on a chunk. This may be by combining different chunks of language or by staring with a chunk and adding some language of one's own. An example could be the following:

A mon avis le poème est très bizarre et il y a des mots bizarres

The very familiar phrases *A mon avis … est … and il y a des …* give the learners the confidence to embark on the creation of their own phrase. These set phrases are called 'utterance launcher[s]' by Thornbury and Slade (2006: 12). Finally, level three is where the learner gets more creative with language:

A mon avis le poème est très amusant et il *me rire* [should be *me fait rire*]

This third level often involves the production of inaccurate language as the learner is trying to express meaning in forms unfamiliar to him or her. This does not mean, however, that this process should be discouraged. It is sometimes tempting to prioritize accuracy above all else but creative construction and the manipulation of language are also important skills to foster. Mitchell (2003: 22) indeed recognizes the importance of creativity and risk-taking to learners' language development.

The view is often advanced that time spent giving learners a basic target language framework with which to talk about literature is time wasted, particularly if, as above, it leads them to use language inaccurately. I would argue, however, that this offers a perfect opportunity to correct language use and give learners the language they need. It may provide a springboard to highlight a particular grammar or vocabulary point. Furthermore, the language used to talk about literature will be in most cases highly transferable to other contexts, such as the GCSE examination, where the giving and justifying of opinions and the use of complex structures are required.

# Removing the support: students give presentations/talks

It is a useful exercise for students to give a short presentation or talk on one aspect of a book – a character, a section of the action, a personal impression. This can be staged gradually, that is, they do their first talk with full notes (reading from a script), building up to detailed written bullet points and then a talk with just written prompts. This serves to improve fluency and confidence, not just in the area of talking about literature but also in their speaking overall.

# Monologues from character's point of view

Students can be encouraged to write a short speech or monologue from a particular character's point of view. This can serve to explain why they have acted as they have or to challenge the actions of another character. This can then be taken further into a more interactive form as a debate.

## Chunks to facilitate discussion of the form of texts

Talk about a text is not limited to the characters and events but can also extend to the form of the text. This may be deemed beyond the competence of early language learners but, also with practice, there is no reason why learners cannot express this in the target language. An example here is the expression of an opinion on the rhyming scheme of a poem:

---

Regardez les derniers mots de chaque ligne. Essayez de les prononcer avec un/e partenaire. Choisissez la bonne rime:

AABBA ABBAA ABAAB

**Partner A:** A mon avis, la bonne rime, c'est ABBAA
**Partner B:** Je ne suis pas d'accord. A mon avis, la bonne rime, c'est AABBA

---

The examples below show a way of further exploring rhymes in the target language. Using the poem Doña pitu piturra by Gloria Fuentes as a stimulus, learners match rhymes for items of clothing:

---

**Partner A:** Creo que un zapato rima con barato
**Partner B:** Estoy de acuerdo. Creo que…

They can also add justifications:

**Partner A:** Creo que un zapato rima con barato porque termina en 'o'
**Partner B:** Estoy de acuerdo. Creo que…

un vestido       negra
una chaqueta     amarillas

---

| | |
|---|---|
| unas zapatillas | bonito |
| una sudadera | anticuados |
| un zapato | rojas |
| unas botas | feo |
| unas botas | marron |
| un vaquero | violeta |
| un pantalón | rotas |
| una camiseta | violeta |
| unos zapatos | barato |
| un zapato | azul-claro |

Other poems which work well for a focus on rhymes are L'Oiseau du Colarado by Robert Desnos and Le Cancre by Jacques Prévert. Le Cancre is a particularly good choice because it incorporates not just rhyme but also repetition, rhythm and alliteration.

## Chunks for production beyond the text

So far, we have looked at how clearly selected language can help with comprehension and production related to understanding of the text. Of course, effective scaffolding of the target language can also enable learners to work creatively *beyond* the text, for example in producing their own versions of the text. Substitution can play an important part here. The original text can act as a stimulus for learners to produce writing of their own, based on that original text.

In the example below, the learners' task is to produce a surreal version of the poem 'La Paloma', initially substituting nouns they know from different topics. Learners enjoy this kind of surreal writing. It has the dual purpose of being creative but also useful for the development of examination skills and related vocabulary.

Se equivocó el/la _____.
Se equivocaba.

Por ir a _____, fue a _____.

Creyó que el/la _____ era el/la_____.
Se equivocaba.

Creyó que el/la _____ era el/la _____;

que el/ la _____ era el/la _____.
Se equivocaba…

A further example below also scaffolds learners in their production of a creative outcome, based on the original poem by Desnos:

Une fourmi de dix-huit mètres
Avec un chapeau sur la tête
Ça n'existe pas ça n'existe pas.

Une fourmi traînant un char
Plein de pingouins et de canards
Ça n'existe pas ça n'existe pas

Une fourmi parlant français
Parlant latin et javanais
Ça n'existe pas ça n'existe pas

Et pourquoi pas?

Learners are then tasked with substituting some of the words to make their own poem. Whereas in the 'La Paloma' example, learners were given picture images to stimulate production, here learners first engage in the activity of categorizing the nouns they are to substitute into the categories of words used in the poem: animals, measures of weight/length, clothes, parts of the body, vehicles, languages, prepositions and verbs. This introduces an element of linguistic analysis into the language learning while also scaffolding the creative process for learners to help them produce an original piece of target language. An example of a list in progress of categories and possible words to substitute is below:

## Remue méninge
### Faites des listes des éléments différents du poème

**1. les animaux**
...une fourmi
...des fourmis

... un pinguin
... des pinguins
... un canard
...des canards

**2. la taille / le poids**
...de dix huit mètres

Il faut regarder dans le glossaire

**3. les vêtements**
...un chapeau

**4. les parties du corps**
...la tête

**7. prépositions**
sur  dans  avec  sans

**5. les véhicules**
... un char

**8. verbes d'action:**
...traîner    ...pousser
        ...porter

**6. les langues**
...français, latin
et javanais

Here is a similar example, without the scaffolding, based on the poem A l'ecole by Jacques Charpentreau:

> Dans notre rue, il y a
> Des _____, des gens qui _____,
> Un_____ magasin, une _____.
> Et puis mon cœur, mon cœur qui bat
> Tout bas

The three types of activity below will also need scaffolding with chunks of language for learners and may well be more suited to more advanced learners.

## Creative writing: letter to the author

A stimulating and motivating context for written work in the target language and in response to the text is a letter to the author. This might respond to some text or quotation where the author has set out his or her intentions with the piece of literature. Alternatively, it may be an evaluative response to the author detailing the emotional impact of the piece and/or questioning certain literary techniques used, the portrayal of certain characters, the way the action or plot unfolds or even suggesting a different ending or twist.

## Creative writing: diary entry by a character

A diary entry is a useful way for students to get inside the personality and motivation of different characters. A diary entry could be written in response to certain events in the book or play or in response to the effect other personalities have on the character writing the entry.

## Creative writing: newspaper/magazine article about a particular event/character

A newspaper or magazine article can be quite versatile because it can consist of narrative, quotations and even speculate on the opinions of others. This is therefore a good way for students to demonstrate their understanding of particular aspects of the text.

# The key role of repetition and practice in the discussion of literature

Once one accepts the need to teach explicitly the target language required to discuss literature, it is still important to recognize that simply teaching it as a one-off is not sufficient. This language – often in the form of chunks or formulas, as seen above – then needs to be automatized, or proceduralized, so that it becomes part of the learners' repertoire, as I have noted previously.

The automatization of these chunks and formulas is given so little focus in standard interpretations of CLT and, indeed, Mitchell (2003: 22) notes the problem of the 'rate of forgetting' due to 'inadequate opportunities to recycle and re-use new language, in meaningful activities'. Myles, Mitchell and Hooper (1999: 75–6) find that, additionally, the automatization of formulaic routines enables learners to 'free up controlled processes' to allow them to focus on form and creative processes.

> Overtime, then, careful planning, repetition activities, scaffolding and the provoking of key structures of language by the teacher can lead to this language becoming internalised by learners such that it then becomes available for spontaneous use. A further aspect of ensuring this language becomes internalised is that it is formally repeated and rehearsed through interactive repetition activities and that the language is displayed via, for example, PowerPoint slides, wall posters, annotations and text written on the board, so that learners have textual support whilst internalising the structures. (Christie, 2017: 81)

Interviews with learners reinforce the view that this frequent exposure and repetition does help them to remember the language. Pupils talk about repetition because it is good to 'get it into your memory', to 'drum everything into our heads', that it 'sticks in your mind' and 'keeps in your head' (Christie, 2011: 284). Arnold, Dornyei and Pugliese (2015: 10) include this notion of automatization and proceduralization as the 'controlled practice principle', one of their seven main principles of the Principled Communicative Approach (PCA).

If, then, learners have not had sufficient time devoted to practice and reinforcement of the language needed to talk about literature, it is very likely that they will switch to English as they will be unable to sustain the conversation. Johnson (1996: 84) points out that the act of speaking uses a certain amount of the brain's 'channel capacity' and that automatized or proceduralized knowledge is fast and light on channel capacity. This means that the brain's channel capacity is freed up to think about the interesting concepts and issues being discussed rather than having to grasp for the language framework required to actually discuss them.

A further benefit of allowing sufficient time for the learner to internalize the language needed is that it provides a boost to confidence and gives the learner a sense of what Ushioda (1996: 32) calls 'communicative success'. This is the sense of being able to say something meaningful in the target language. So often in the languages classroom, especially in the early stages, even if learners get this sense, it is likely to be in quite transactional or mundane language contexts. The beauty of literature is they get the satisfaction of being able to communicate concepts and feelings which go beyond the everyday at an early stage in their language learning career.

# Repetition to build confidence and understanding

So often, learners can be exposed to a text but are not given the time to get to know it more intimately. Reading it over and over can help with this familiarization with the text but producing it out loud is also a very effective way to embed it in the memory. Simply reciting it around the room, in the form of a game of dominoes, can work well. Each learner can be given a line of a poem, for example, and the poem can be displayed on the board. The first person reads the first line, then each learner has to say his or her line in turn. A competitive element can be added such that the class sees how quickly it can complete the whole poem.

A paired dictation can also work well. Below is an example, again with the poem 'La Paloma'. Ideally, students sit back to back (to avoid their simply copying from each other). Person B starts with the word 'Se', then person A says 'equivocó' and so on so that learners each complete their version using the words provided from their partner.

---

PAIR DICTATION (PARTNER A)

____ equivocó __ paloma.

___equivocaba.

____ ir __ norte, ____ al _____.

Creyó _____ el _____ era _____.

Se _____.

Creyó ____ el _____ era ___ cielo;

____ la _____, la _____.

Se _____.

Que _____ estrellas, _____;

que _____ calor; ____ nevada.

_____equivocaba.

_____ tu _____ era ____ blusa;

_____tu _____, su _____.

Se _____.

(Ella ____ durmió ___ la _____.

Tú, ____ la _____ de _____ rama.)

PAIR DICTATION (PARTNER B)

Se _____ la _____.

Se _____.

Por ____ al _____, fue ____ sur.

_____que ____ trigo _____ agua.

_____equivocaba.

_____ que ___ mar _____ el _____;

que ____ noche, _____mañana.

_____ equivocaba.

_____ las _____, rocío;

_____ la _____; la _____.

Se _____.

Que____ falda _____ tu _____;

que ____ corazón, _____ casa.

_____ equivocaba.

(_____ se _____ en ___ orilla.

_____, en ____ cumbre ____ una _____.)

---

# Repetition to facilitate production of opinions about characters and events

There is, of course, a whole range of repetition and practice activities which can be used for the language with which to talk about literature. Some examples are given below based on the following sample PowerPoint slide. This sample is in English but should of course be in the relevant target language. The slide helps to drill different opinions in the target language.

How do you find the main character?

| Picture | | |
|---|---|---|
| 1 I think he is cruel | 2 I think he is funny | 3 I think he is strange |

| Picture | | |
|---|---|---|
| 4 I think he is ambitious | 5 I think he is generous | 6 I think he is impatient |

| Picture | | |
|---|---|---|
| 7 I think he is arrogant | 8 I think he is friendly | 9 I think he is jealous |

Activities based on the above slide:

1  Test your partner pairwork
   Person A looks at the slide, Person B tries not to look:
   **A:** How do you find the main character (number 6)?
   **B:** I think he is impatient.
   **A:** That is correct. How do you find the main character (number 4)?
   **B:** I think he is ambitious.
   **A:** That is not correct.

2  First to say
   The teacher asks the question and then flashes up one of the phrases. The first partner in each pair to shout it out gains a point.

3  Secret choice
   The teacher (or a student) chooses and writes down one of the phrases. A student has to guess which one. A maximum of three guesses is allowed.
   **Teacher:**   How do you find the main character?
   **Student:**   I think he is cruel.
   **Teacher:**   That is not correct.
   This can then be done in pairs.

4  Mastermind
   The teacher (or a student) chooses three of the phrases. A student has to say the correct three.
   **Teacher:**   How do you find the main character?
   **Student:**   I think he is cruel, I think he is friendly, I think he is ambitious.

**Teacher:**    One correct
This can then be done in pairs.

**5** Coloured sentences

This examples drills the language needed for students to predict what the text is about, perhaps from a book cover or associated image or the title. They work in pairs and the partner can agree/disagree in the target language. For students to practise the phrases, the activity shown is one of coloured sentences; the teacher says a sentence and learners have to say the colour before the teacher reaches the end of the sentence. This can then be done in pairs.

Je crois que le texte va parler du pauvreté
Je crois que le texte va parler du sport
Je crois que le texte va parler de la politique
Je crois que le texte va parler de l'adolescence
Je crois que le texte va parler des enfants
Je crois que le texte va parler des sans-abris

Other useful activities are ones which feature regularly in foreign language classrooms, for example, trap door, battleships, noughts and crosses:

# Trap door

One student leaves the room. The rest of the class decides on the chosen answer for each question. The student then returns. The class asks each question in turn. The student answers. If the student chooses the 'correct' answer, the class goes on and asks the next question. If not, they ask the question again. Each time the student gets an answer wrong, the class goes back to the first question again.

How do you find the main character?

    1  I think he is cruel.
    2  I think he is funny.
    3  I think he is strange.

What does he look like?

    1  He seems young.
    2  He seems ill.
    3  He seems tired.

What will happen to him in the end?

    1  I think he will get married.
    2  I think he will leave the country.
    3  I think he will stay.

## Battleships

This game can be played with literature-related language instead of the more usual topic language:

| In my opinion, the action will take place: | | | | | | |
|---|---|---|---|---|---|---|
| in France | | | | | | |
| in the USA | | | | | | |
| in the UK | | | | | | |
| in Chile | | | | | | |
| in Germany | | | | | | |
| in Morocco | | | | | | |
| | in a city | in a town | in a village | by the sea | in the country | in the mountains |

# Literature as context: applying the principles of encouraging learner target language use to the study of literature

My study into the conditions which promote spontaneous classroom talk among learners (Christie, 2017) identified context as a significant factor, supported by an element of competition and reward.

An important aspect of encouraging target language use among learners is the creation of a context which stimulates them sufficiently to communicate in the target language. This careful attention to the context of the talk I have called context management:

> 'context management' … involves the teacher's creation of a context which is rich enough to stimulate spontaneous talk. (Christie, 2017: 84)

In my original study, the context of the learner talk is the classroom where learners are incentivized to talk about each other and events as they unfold in the typical routines of classroom life. Coupled with judicious rewards and mildly competitive activities, this context motivates learners to use the target language in spontaneous and often creative ways. The driving force behind this context is its immediate and concrete nature and its ability to provoke reactions on the spot. These reactions are usually rooted in emotional responses, such as frustration, disappointment or protest if a student or a team is losing in a competitive environment. It might be surprise at a turn of events or laughter in response to someone else's comments. All these emotions can form the basis of verbal communication in the target language.

The beauty of literature is its ability to create contexts through its well-drawn characters, settings and narrative of events. These can serve as a stimulus for target language talk in the same way as the classroom setting if their contexts are made real for the learner. As noted above, a key element which motivates spontaneous target language talk is if the context and hence the talk is invested with emotion strong enough to make the learner want to speak in the first place. Van Lier links emotion with agency, that is the 'taking hold' of language for one's own purposes:

> The notion of agency requires that the learner invest physical, mental and emotional energy in the language produced. (van Lier, 2008: 178)

Literary texts represent the ideal context for the generation of agency and communication invested with emotion and creativity.

---

### Research summary

Coffey (2016) explores the notion of creativity in relation to the teaching of literature. He points out how creativity has come into vogue in recent years and the benefits it can bring to language learning in general. He is against the notion of language and literature as separate components and argues for their integration. He points out how pleasing it is to see literature for enjoyment and as a source of creativity back on the agenda in the National Curriculum. Coffey identifies the following arguments for using literature for pedagogic purposes, which should guide the teacher's choice of text: an authentic model of language, a cultural artefact and a resource for studying the aesthetic dimension of the language. He includes a case study of a teacher who has worked on *Le Petit Prince* (Saint-Exupéry, 1943) with her Year 7 class. The teacher explored the characters with her learners and engaged them on an emotional level, 'drawing them in' (91).

Coffey concludes that work with a literary text operates on many levels: enjoyment of the rhythm and musicality of children's stories, the potential to develop empathy and the exploration of universal themes.

### Reflections on the research

1 Try to find short poems which might particularly appeal to the emotions and explore universal themes.
2 Can you list some basic phrases in the target language you teach, which learners might need to express emotional responses to a poem or short piece of literature?

---

The key stage 3 and 4 curriculum can so often be based around transactional language and descriptions of one's own routine, and exposure to more creative work can make a refreshing change. Literature, however, opens up a whole area of content beyond the transactional. As Diamantidaki notes,

> The reader can explore the thoughts, feelings, beliefs and fears of a population of a particular context and start making links with their own reality. This is just as powerful as engaging with contexts that might deal with the more immediate concerns of learners. (2016: 57–58)

It is argued here that it is not just in comprehension that one can engage with these dimensions but also in the production of the target language. Learners can reuse and reframe language from texts to give their own opinions and express their own feelings. Indeed, this is not necessarily at odds with what is required in external examinations, required to express personal responses here too.

Diamantidaki (2016), referencing Widdowson, points out how the appreciation of literature is a process of relating to the contexts and attitudes on display. This mirrors Horne's analysis of authentic communication in the target language. She describes it as 'a two-way process', involving 'an interactional relationship' and containing 'personal emotion or thought' (2014: 67). This reinforces how appropriate it is to give expression to one's experience of literature by doing so in the target language.

First, learners can have an emotional response, expressed in the target language, to the characters and events in a text. If well managed by the teacher, learners will express and debate a number of differing responses to individual characters and events. As already seen above, learners can speculate about characters and events and offer opinions on different personalities. If they have the simple language of agreement and disagreement, they can invest their discussions with feeling:

---

A ton avis, de quoi va parler le texte?
Je crois que le texte va parler de…
Je crois que le texte ne va pas parler de…
Je suis d'accord!
Je ne suis pas d'acord!

The language to develop and express emotions further can also be taught:
Tu plaisantes!
Das darf nicht wahr sein!
Estas bromeando!

---

Second, the characters and events themselves can form the context to promote target language talk. Learners can take on roles and develop scripts in character. They can also debate, even in simple terms, how a plot might develop or how or why a character will act/acted.

# Dialogues/role plays

One way of getting students to interact on an emotional level with the characters in the text is to set up a dialogue or role play based around one particular event in the text. This may be an event which is simply described and students can put their own dialogue to this event. Alternatively, it may be an incident that is simply implied and again students can invent what happened in the form of a dialogue. Furthermore, it could be that students imagine a dialogue that may have happened before a particular incident or after it. This can be taken further with the inclusion of a dramatic interpretation, as learners act out a dialogue or interpretation of events.

# Debates

While a dialogue or role play can be situated very much in the reality of the action of the text or play, a debate can focus a bit more abstractly on the actions that characters have taken. This could be set up where, for example, individual characters justify their reasons for acting as they did in a certain situation and other characters challenge them, even if they are characters who were not present in a particular event. As learners progress through key stages 4 and 5, the language of debate can increase in complexity:

| **Je suis contre cette idée/ solution.** | **I'm opposed to that proposal.** |
| --- | --- |
| Je ne pense pas que ce soit la meilleure façon d'aborder le problème. | I don't think it's the best way to deal with the problem |
| Je suis d'accord dans une certaine mesure, mais en revanche … | I agree up to a point, but on the other hand … |
| Etant donné que/ vu que … | Because/since/seeing that/given that … |
| Ce serait de la folie de … | It would be madness to … |
| Cela ne me semble pas être la bonne manière de s'attaquer au problème. | That doesn't seem to me to be the right way to tackle the problem. |
| Cela n'est pas toujours le cas. | That's not always the case. |
| Ce que vous proposez risque de … | What you propose runs the risk of … |
| Un autre aspect du problème, c'est que … | Another aspect of the problem is … |
| Loin de résoudre le problème, cela pourrait … | Far from solving the problem, that could … |
| Je ne suis pas du tout d'accord avec vous là-dessus. | I don't agree with you at all on that. |
| Il faut se rappeler que … | It must be remembered that… |
| Je suis opposé(e) à cette proposition. | I'm opposed to that proposal. |
| La société actuelle ne peut plus tolérer … | Present day society can no longer tolerate… |
| Il faut bien reconnaître que … | It must be recognized that… |
| Selon moi, c'est une politique/ mesure vouée à l'échec. | In my opinion that policy/ measure is bound to fail. |
| Je vois les choses tout à fait différemment. | I see things quite differently. |
| Je ne partage pas votre point de vue. | I don't share your point of view. |

From: *Advancing Oral Skills*, Anneli McLachlan, APF1

In terms of the element of competition, a competitive aspect need not be excluded here either. For example, these small-scale debates over what may happen next or on the nature of different characters can be set up so that the most convincing argument wins. Competition can also be incorporated into the techniques for learning and practising the language needed to talk about literature, as seen earlier.

Tangible reward has also been identified as a driver for successful spontaneous classroom communication (Christie, 2017). In my study, these rewards were immediate and simple, usually in the form of points for short utterances produced totally spontaneously. In the case of literature, such instant rewards could have a place. They could also be given for more extended pieces of oral and written work such as dialogues, presentations and posters.

---

*Reflective activity*

*Aim:* To reflect upon the target language needs of learners when talking and writing about literature.

*Evidence and reflection:* Think of the different aspects of a literary text which learners will need to talk about: the author, the setting, the characters, the plot (what happened, what might happen next, what might have happened), opinions about the text (emotional and more objective responses) and justifications of those opinions. There are also aspects which would enable learners to talk about the text as a piece of literature, for example, rhyme scheme for a poem and narrative voice for a novel.

Make a list, in the languages you teach, of the target language structures and vocabulary, that learners will need to be taught in order to talk about these areas.

*Extension:* Some argue that it is a waste of time talking about literature in the target language. Look at the relevant examination specification (GCSE or A level in the UK) and see how the language used in terms of discussing literature is transferable to other topics and examination question types.

---

*Checklist*

*Aim:* To consider the vital ingredients for the successful exploration in the target language of literature.

- Ensure learners are taught the target language they need to respond to and discuss a text.
- Include a range of activities to aid with comprehension:
  - Multiple-choice activities
  - Putting events in the correct order
  - True/false
- Ensure a range of interactive activities is included:
  - Back-to-back dictation
  - Quiz, quiz, trade
- Explore the form of the text, not just the meaning, for example, rhyme scheme.
- Give full scope for emotional responses to the text and opinions (of characters, for example).
- Allow learners space to explore creative responses, for example, writing their own poem.

# Conclusion

It is hoped that this chapter has not only provided a rationale for using the target language to explore literary texts but also provided some useful ways of approaching this. Once learners have been taught the language they need, they can then become more confident with it as they practise and use it. They will be able to transfer such language to other contexts and also to adapt language from other contexts. Finally, a focus on using the language to express emotions and opinions related to literary texts can be a real motivating factor which encourages and rewards authentic language use.

# References

AQA. (2016a online). 'GCSE French'. Available at http://www.aqa.org.uk/subjects/languages/gcse/french-8658.

AQA. (2016b online). 'A Level French'. Available at http://www.aqa.org.uk/subjects/languages/as-and-a-level/french-7652.

Arnold, J., Z. Dornyei and C. Pugliese. (2015). *The Principled Communicative Approach*. London: Helbling Languages.

Camus. A. (1988). *L'Étranger*. London: Routledge.

Christie, C. (2011). 'Speaking Spontaneously: An Examination of the University of Cumbria Approach to the Teaching of Modern Foreign Languages'. Unpublished PhD thesis.

Christie, C. (2017). 'Speaking Spontaneously in the Modern Foreign Languages Classroom: Tools for Supporting Successful Target Language Conversation'. *Language Learning Journal*, 4(1): 74–89.

Coffey, S. (2016). 'Teaching Literature to Promote Creativity in Language Learning'. In C. Christie and C. Conlon (Eds), *Success Stories from Secondary Foreign Languages Classrooms: Models from London School Partnerships with Universities*. London: Trentham Books at UCL Press.

Crichton, H. (2009). ' "Value Added" Modern Languages Teaching in the Classroom: An Investigation into How Teachers' Use of Classroom Target Language Can Aid Pupils' Communication Skills'. *Language Learning Journal*, 37 (1): 19–34.

Department for Education (DfE). (2013). *Modern Foreign Languages in the National Curriculum*. London: HMSO.

Diamantidaki, F. (2016). 'Using Literature in the Key Stage 3 Modern Foreign Languages Classroom'. In C. Christie and C. Conlon (Eds), *Success Stories from Secondary Foreign Languages Classrooms: Models from London School Partnerships with Universities*. London: Trentham Books at UCL Press.

Ellis, R. (2008). *The Study of Second Language Acquisition*. Oxford: Oxford University Press.

Horne, K. (2014). 'Speaking Interactively'. In P. Driscoll, E. Macaro and A. Swarbrick (Eds), *Debates in Modern Languages Education*. London: Routledge.

Macaro, E. (2000). 'Issues in Target Language Teaching'. In K. Field (Ed.), *Issues in Modern Foreign Languages Teaching*, 171–89. Abingdon: Routledge.

McLachlan, A. (2011). *Advanced Pathfinder 1: Advancing Oral Skills*. London: CILT.

Mitchell, R. (2003). 'Rethinking the Concept of Progression in the National Curriculum for Modern Foreign Languages: A Research Perspective'. *Language Learning Journal*, 27: 15–23.

Myles, F., R. Mitchell and J. Hooper (1999). 'Interrogative Chunks in French L2: A Basis for Creative Construction?' *Studies in Second Language Acquisition*, 21: 49–81.

Pachler, N. and D. Allford. (2000). 'Literature in the Communicative Classroom'. In K. Field (Ed.), *Issues in Modern Foreign Languages Teaching*. London: Routledge.

Saint-Exupéry, A. de (1943). *Le Petit Prince*. Paris: Gallimard. With thanks to Ciara Mulvenna: Le Petit Nicolas materials; Lisa Panford: La Paloma activities; Marian Carty: Robert Desnos activities; Alyssa Hickson: Doña pitu piturra exercise.

Thornbury, S. and D. Slade. (2006). *Conversation: From Description to Pedagogy*. Cambridge: Cambridge University Press.

Ushioda, E. (1996). *Learner Autonomy: The Role of Motivation*, vol. 5. Dublin: Authentik.

van Lier, L. (2008). 'Agency in the Classroom'. In J. P. Lantolf and M. E. Poehner (Eds), *Sociocultural Theory and the Teaching of Second Languages*, 163–86. London: Equinox.

# 8

# Teachers Supporting Teachers

*Steven Fawkes*

## Introduction

This chapter describes the context which prompted the Association for Language Learning (ALL) members to create a collaborative wiki focused on teachers' thoughts about exploiting literature and authentic texts. It then explores the creation of content and development of classroom strategies which result in the ALL Literature wiki.

*ALL is the largest membership association for language teachers in the UK and works to support the professional lives of language teaching professionals* (ALL, 2018).

The newest version of the National Curriculum (NC) as it applies to England, introduced in 2014 (DfE, NC, 2014), marked considerable change for many teachers, in both primary and secondary sectors. The Schools Minister Nick Gibb in Simons and Porter (2015) refers to it as a Knowledge Curriculum and priority is given to facts (e.g. in history) and to terminology and accuracy (e.g. in grammar and spelling in English).

For teachers of languages (modern foreign languages, or MFL in curriculum terms, form a statutory part of the National Curriculum in key stages 2 and 3 (DfE, 2013)), the new requirements focused, or refocused, teachers' attention on several elements which presented challenges for their schemes of work: a return to translations (in both directions), an emphasis on spontaneity in speaking, and extension in writing, explicit requirements in the field of grammar and the inclusion of the words 'great literature' (DfE, NC Archives, 2013) (viz. *Purpose of study* below).

## The main challenges

Why were some of these concepts challenging? Largely because, for many younger teachers in the profession some of these features had not been integral to their own training; indeed, some of them may not have been given priority in their own learning of their language.

From the early years of the National Curriculum onwards (the 1990s), there was a strong overall emphasis on communication (NC); this did not, of course, exclude the development of grammatical knowledge – grammar is an essential part of effective communication and was referred to – but it did tend to sideline it in teachers' planning of their busy schemes of work. Likewise, external exams since that period have no longer included exercises in translation (in either direction) and as a result this had become not only less present in lessons but sometimes also controversial in terms of a communicative philosophy. Finally, far from requiring spontaneity, the version of the GCSE speaking test in place until the most recent changes gave most weight to prepepared oral work in a controlled assessment model in which students could script and learn by heart their spoken presentations.

The case of literature is similarly remote from many younger teachers' experiences, especially in the context of key stages 3 and 4, as noted by Dobson (2018) who comments on the curriculum 'Striking new elements are the introduction of translation and "literature" (as opposed to general reference to written texts). This presents a new challenge for almost all teachers, since most now have little experience of teaching translation and literature below the sixth form (ages 16–18).'

Although there had in recent iterations of the curriculum been an emphasis on encountering authentic materials, these tended for a period to be more functional, transactional documents (advertisements, brochures, menus, catalogues, etc.) than especially literary. Indeed many of the texts used for teaching and learning were often specially created by authors of course materials or by teachers themselves, in order to control the language level and content. One exception to this pattern would be the inclusion of letters and other correspondence, often exploited as linguistic models for pupils to adapt.

Another exception, albeit more in the primary sector than the secondary, and developed alongside the primary initiatives around the turn of the millennium, would be the inclusion of stories as language and culture-focused texts.

## Reflection

What would be the advantages, for teachers planning a lesson or scheme to work, to limit the range of texts to those specially created in their course materials?

What would be the advantages of including in such plans a wide range of authentic texts, intended for native speakers, such as literary works?

For languages in key stage 2 and for key stage 3, the National Curriculum Purpose of Study for MFL says,

Learning a foreign language is a liberation from insularity and provides an opening to other cultures. A high-quality languages education should foster pupils' curiosity and deepen their understanding of the world (DfE 2013, 1).

It goes on to stress the need for learners' opportunities to speak spontaneously, 'express their ideas and thoughts in another language and to understand and respond to its speakers, both in speech and in writing' and to use the language learning experience to 'learn new ways of thinking and read great literature in the original language'. These statements in particular were to provide a focus for the work of the ALL Literature project as it developed.

Of course, some teachers had always enjoyed integrating authentic texts and short literary works of different genres in their lessons for different purposes – but this approach was not generalized; literary texts did not form part of examinations at that point, and their relevance to teenage learners was not obvious.

As the elements of the curriculum began to look more technical (with accuracy being highlighted and translation coming to the fore), teachers became concerned about their recruitment of students after key stage 3, when languages become optional, and the possible impact on examination data. It was in response to this challenge that volunteers on the ALL Council identified the need to support colleagues in very practical ways, particularly in relation to the concept of literature (its nature and its exploitation in the languages classroom) and more generally in relation to tying all aspects of the new Programme of Study (PoS) into a coherent whole which would stimulate learners and teachers alike, support progression and promote motivation for language learning in the longer term.

There has historically been a perceived risk that the separate elements of the curriculum be seen as separate teaching objectives by teachers, and hence by learners, so that lessons might be broken up artificially into a section for listening, one for speaking, one for cultural learning, one for writing, one for reading and Office for Standards in Education (OFSTED, 2015) has observed uneven attention being given to some areas, especially that of reading and authentic materials. These observations would contribute to the formulation of a conceptual framework.

Since the inception of a National Curriculum, the intention has usually been that the curriculum should form a whole, should go beyond subject boundaries and should make a holistic educational experience. (Indeed at certain points in the history of the national curriculum, there have been cross-curricular themes and dimensions which have made links explicit both between subjects and with wider life skills, especially when the National Curriculum applied also to languages in key stage 4). All of these intentions are now encapsulated in the very brief Purpose of Study which introduces the Languages Programme of Study within the UK National Curriculum.

## Reflection

What would you identify as the key messages of the Purpose of Study?

How would you plan to convey your chosen messages to learners in the age ranges you work with?

- in key stage 2?
- in key stage 3?
- at the crucial point of making options decisions at the end of key stage 3?

As a languages teacher my priority is to engage my learners, and I would consequently place significant value on the motivational aspects I identify in the Purpose of Study above: selecting authentic resources in a range of media in order to *foster pupils' curiosity*, encouraging interaction within and beyond the classroom to *enable pupils to express their ideas and thoughts, … understand and respond, … communicate for practical purposes* and accessing texts which introduce the cultural dimension of *new ways of thinking*.

Devising learning activities and teaching plans to sustain these positive messages will rely on the teacher's understanding of what motivates learners at different ages, and *reading great literature in the original language* presents specific challenges, not least in respect to the age-appropriateness of the original literary text, which was almost certainly not written for teenage readers. Identifying appropriate and engaging texts thus became a key strand in the ALL Literature project.

The teacher is further faced with the challenge of integrating the elements detailed in the Subject Content of the PoS (following on from the Purpose of Study) and combining them, in a sensible and subtle way, so that a single learning activity may touch on more than one of them at once. This is simply for pragmatic reasons of time availability but also serves to show learners that the language is a whole.

An example might be that learners explore an authentic text (or piece of literature) to develop their vocabulary, and/or to express ideas and opinions, and/or to begin to learn about translation, and/or to observe a useful grammatical detail.

The teachers' skill here lies in balancing the diverse elements of a scheme of work (vocabulary, grammar, phonic awareness, language skills, etc.), with awareness of learners' literacy level and their conceptual, emotional and linguistic development, and selecting or devising appropriate resources.

The PoS (DfE 2013, 1) goes on to suggest how literature and authentic texts contribute substantially to learning:

> The National Curriculum for languages aims to ensure that all pupils:
> *understand and respond to spoken and written language from a variety of authentic sources.*

The implication may be that this engagement with 'real life' is motivating, and the clear message is that learners should be taught the skills and strategies to help them 'understand' – which may sometimes mean getting the gist and sometimes the detail – and to respond.

> Speak with increasing confidence, fluency and spontaneity, finding ways of communicating what they want to say, including through discussion and asking questions, and continually improving the accuracy of their pronunciation and intonation.

There is no explicit link here with texts, but there is a positive message about the primacy offered within this version of the curriculum to **Authenticity** and **Spontaneity**, which teachers can usefully consider as two sides of the same coin – authentic texts and authentic language/spontaneous response in authentic communication.

Also, given the time limitations within the curriculum, it may well be that learners will gain some of the language and the skills they need from sources beyond their class teacher, just as they may well acquire the variety and depth of language suggested in the next statement from wider reading, viewing and listening:

> Can write at varying length, for different purposes and audiences, using the variety of grammatical structures that they have learnt, discover and develop an appreciation of a range of writing in the language studied.

The concept of 'range' was helpful in informing the work of the ALL Literature project and development of the ALL Literature wiki, as it opened up thinking about what extent of writing, authentic text or literary text is appropriate to learners of school age as they proceed towards an encounter with 'great literature', and how a range of texts would contribute to the wider aims of the languages curriculum.

## Reflection

How could you as a teacher, or as a department, encapsulate the philosophy of your scheme of work in words that would make sense to learners, parents, governors or senior leaders? What is the ethos you are trying to create?

# The strategies 1: what were the challenges?

In summary, the challenges faced by the ALL Literature project were at this point:

To bring together a project group

To develop a conceptual framework to support teachers which would embrace the specific requirements of the National Curriculum (and consequently developments in external examinations), a broader shared professional rationale for including authentic texts and literature in language lessons and advice on integrating the literature element with the other elements of a scheme of work

To identify texts from a diversity of sources which could be interesting for school-aged pupils

To indicate strategies for exploiting these texts which fit within the Purpose of Study and serve the Aims of the PoS.

The ALL Council set up a working group of members around the country from different sectors and backgrounds by invitation, through ALL's weekly electronic newsletter (ALLnet) sent to all its members; any teachers interested in supporting this development work could join an inclusive and informal group, which would operate largely at a distance. Early discussions focused on teachers' anxieties, with the words 'great literature' raising further questions.

Why consider integrating Literature into Language lessons? What is great literature? If it is only famous poetry and prose, how does that relate to age-appropriateness? Most great literature was, after all, written for adults (which language learners in key stage 3 are not) with adult literary themes and in adult language, which language learners are very unlikely to reach in key stage 3.

## Window on research

A checklist of reasons to use Literature in the Languages classroom is included in *Why Teach Literature in the Foreign Language Classroom?* Jonathan P. A. Sell Universidad de Alcalá, Encuentro 15, 2005, *Journal of Research and Innovation in the Language Classroom*, in Section 2. The case for literature.

https://ebuah.uah.es/dspace/bitstream/handle/10017/573/11_Sell.pdf?sequence=1

Before consulting the list, consider these questions:

What do you think the reasons will be?

After consulting the list, consider the reasons again; do you agree? Which are most relevant to your classes?

Third, schools, teachers and pupils in classes are all individual in their tastes, behaviours and motivations. In your own context, what would you include under the heading 'Literature for the classroom' and why?

ALL has extensive online communications network via fora and social media, and our first decision was to ask members these very questions through a survey; the responses were, as ever, pragmatic and forward-looking: they centred on the professional knowledge that teachers have of their learners. Classroom resources, in whatever medium, need to be accessible, and to recognize the stage of development (linguistic and intellectual) of the learners. That is not to say that learners need to have complete familiarity with every word involved in a text, but that they do need to understand at least enough to make it interesting, and they do need strategies to help them realize what they do understand.

One contributor to the ALL survey wrote, 'Literature does not have to be long, complicated or difficult – but it can give students a real sense of achievement and empowerment to have understood a song / poem / simple story or part of a story and then to adapt it and create their own version. It uses language for a real reason and with an audience in mind, which gives the whole exercise of language learning a legitimacy and purpose.'

Another said, 'To be successful in class, any text has to be age-appropriate either in terms of its content or in terms of the activity you do with it.'

Beyond these sensible observations, colleagues noted that the PoS was not defining the sorts of text (just as it does not define any specific content or approaches), preferring to leave the choice to the teachers; in consequence, teachers who responded provided suggestions of what they were already using (or planning to use) and suggestions of other authentic texts which they know their learners respond to, and which they considered could fit the heading 'Literature'. The responses reflect a very broad interpretation of the term.

Literature =

short stories, news articles, songs
adverts, posters, magazine articles
publications, scenes from plays

poetry/song lyrics
poem forms such as 'haiku, Elfchen, luunes, fairy tales / Maerchen
rhymes, tongue twisters
letters
myths and legends
cartoon strips, comics
proverbs, jokes
and even film clips
(accessed from http://all-literature.wikidot.com/what-is-literature)

Why do teachers include all of these elements within the same heading? Because they use their classroom experience to interpret 'Literature' as meaning authentic text for different audiences and crucially because they find, in actual classroom practice, that all of these types of 'literature' elicit a response from learners.

This response can be in the form of one or more of these desirable outcomes:

- The acquisition of some new, wider vocabulary
- The use of the target language for expressing views
- The identification of relevant linguistic features, for example, grammatical forms
- Specific linguistic skills such as gist/detail comprehension or spot translation
- Recycling into a new piece of writing or oral production

Several of these aspects are also prescribed elsewhere in the PoS, of course.

Under *Grammar and vocabulary* is the statement 'develop and use a wide-ranging and deepening vocabulary' which, in the context of a piece of literature, is what learners can be taught to pick out, in order to use it themselves at relevant moments.

The aim around *Linguistic competence* suggests learners 'listen to a variety of forms of spoken language' which supports our interpretation of literature as being more than written text and goes on to suggest they 'read and show comprehension of original and adapted materials from a range of different sources, understanding the purpose, important ideas and details' which helps teachers target learner engagement through real-life experiences as well as linguistic range.

Finally this section of the PoS requires learners to 'write creatively to express their own ideas and opinions' – a creative use of language, for which learners need both models of how people write, and extended language which can be recycled or adapted within their own writing. These are available, of course, within authentic texts which are also, in themselves, highly appropriate for stimulating the expression of views by learners.

The working group next considered suggesting a range of criteria for teachers to use in the selection of interesting and useful literary texts; these included

- the literary quality of the works.
- the accessibility of the texts (linguistically and in practical terms of availability).
- a balance between culturally valued classics (Great Literature) and contemporary works.
- diversity of styles, formats, etc.
- the potential pedagogic and educational practices they allow.

While discussion within the group was generally in accord with such ideas, the point was made that language teachers have very little time available to research texts anyway and may not require such prescriptive parameters. They often have pragmatic and short-term reasons for making choices of text, which are based on personal taste and their knowledge of their own classes.

## Reflection

What are they key points you identify for yourself to bear in mind when selecting a text for a class?
What sorts of authentic texts should we introduce our learners to?
Why are they relevant?
What aspects of these texts could we exploit?
What sorts of activity are age-/development-appropriate in different classes?

# The strategies 2: what forms of support?

The working group identified early on that one way of proceeding which stood a chance of success was to collate ideas, suggestions and recommendations from practising teachers as well as carrying out desk research on literature-related themes; the collaborative and mutually supportive ethos of the ALL also suggested that a good format for the collected work would be a wiki, where teachers could join, read, review and add their own thoughts over time. The group bid successfully through ALL for some development funding from the Fédération Internationale des Professeurs de Français (FIPF)and sought out a colleague to join the group who was already familiar with setting up a wiki.

He asked the group to identify the contents and navigation they would require; these contents have evolved over time but now consist of:

- introduction to the wiki – a short user guide.
- what is our rationale?
- what is literature?
- pedagogy and research – documentation from publications and conferences.
- curriculum starting points.
- advice on using literature in the classroom – getting started.
- background reading.
- online sources of texts – a digest of weblinks to international sites featuring interesting short texts.
- culture for teachers – a page with links intended to be of interest to non-specialist teachers in the primary sector.

(accessed from http://ALL-Literature.wikidot.com)

Central to the home page are the Book Boxes in specific languages, where teachers' contributions are stored.

The working group was clear from an early point that providing a list of texts was not sufficient for busy teachers; to be blunt, many of them would not find time to explore the lists, never mind devise classroom activities alongside them.

We therefore met to compile a pro forma which contributors complete when submitting their suggestions; this asks for details such as the language (which serves to sort the contribution into the relevant Book Box), the title and author and availability of the work suggested and an outline of the teacher's suggested approaches, that is, how the teacher used, or would use, the text with a class. This proved very effective in engaging contributors and inspiring their professional sharing.

Worked example of the pro forma:

| | |
|---|---|
| Contributor | Steven Fawkes |
| Language | Spanish |
| Text | Traditional verse |
| **Title** | La llave de Roma |
| **Intended age of pupils** | **KS2/3 – Year 5–7** |
| **References** – Where can you find the text? A URL? A book? Please give as full a reference as possible. | https://www.youtube.com/watch?v=YlnpGDQhmwM<br>*Extract:*<br>*En Roma hay una calle;*<br>*En la calle una casa;*<br>*Adentro de la casa una cocina*<br>*Cerca de la cocina una sala . . .* |
| **Accompanying resources – including** Teaching resources you have made and can contribute | n/a |
| **Approaches & related activities –** What do you want to do with it? | This text is read in Spanish quite slowly, and in short sentences which are accessible and supported visually in separate scenes. It lends itself to a sequence of activities (potentially over several lessons) for different skills.<br>(A) Listening/Speaking / (Writing):<br>1 The learners watch the first few (four?) scenes for understanding<br>2 The teacher begins to recite from the beginning, pausing and asking the whole class to contribute the next word or words:<br>*En Roma hay una calle;*<br>*En la calle una ...?*<br>This can be used to reinforce the gender marker link *una* + a feminine word<br>3 The teacher checks that learners understand the prepositions of place through spot translation |

4  The teacher shows the same scenes again with the sound off and asks the class to read/recall the Spanish with good pronunciation

5  The learners work in groups to recall the scenes in speech (and/or, if relevant, in writing)

6  The teacher plays the scenes again with sound and moves on to the next group of scenes, asking different groups to remember the new sentences

7  The teacher begins to recite from the beginning, pausing and asking the groups to contribute the next word or words

8  The learners work in groups to recall the extended scenes in speech

9  The teacher organizes the class game 'I went to market . . .' Learners take it in turn to recall: sentence 1, sentence 1 + 2; sentence 1 + 2 + 3 etc. and add other sentences when they reach the end

10  Learners invent their own version of the verse in writing, using short sentences, *hay,* and prepositions, but maybe a different context than the house and furniture

11  The teacher plays more of the scenes (with the sound off) and asks the class, or individuals to read the sentences aloud with good pronunciation (identifying any misunderstandings to address later on)
(B) Reading/Translation

1  The teacher presents on screen (or on paper) the sentences from the scenes in a random order; learners use their reading skills to sequence them and then translate them

2  The teacher presents an edited version of the same sentences – with the prepositions changed – and asks learners how they would adapt their translations

| | |
|---|---|
| **Rationale** – Why do you want to do it? | To develop pupils' memorizing skill<br>To support speaking and phonics recognition<br>To introduce, and practise use of, prepositions of place |
| **Outcomes** – What does the student produce as a result? | Spoken performances<br>Written sentences using a structure and grammatical elements |
| Related **teaching topics** – How does it fit in your scheme? | Vocabulary: Rooms in the house<br>Prepositions |
| Related **grammar topics** you highlight | Hay<br>Revisiting gender of nouns<br>Prepositions |
| **Key words** – List two or three words in the Language and in English to help others search | Hay<br>Prepositions |
| *Generic Language learning strategies* | Listening to a verse / performing a verse<br>Personal creative writing |
| **Time Frame** – How long does it take? | Around 40 minutes, but can be split up or extended |
| Anything else?<br>Details of copyright? | The resource is online |

When contributors click on 'Click here to make a new entry', they see this pro forma in a refined form; they are not obliged to fill in every detail, but the extent of some of their contributions, especially in respect of their own teaching materials, is remarkably generous: there are examples of worksheets, short presentation files, lesson plans and lesson presentation sequences and even extensive schemes of work. This genuinely is 'teachers supporting teachers'.

Another element the group identified as being of major importance to busy teachers is the Search function at the top of the screen; this is powerful and can select relevant items based on search words. These could be teacherly terms such as grammar points or age-references, or vocabulary items or themes (family, countries, genre, etc.)

## Reflection

What are the key points in the process of creating the Literature wiki that strike you? What elements do you think may be missing from the strategy?

By far the largest area of the Literature wiki is that of **Online sources of texts** where there are hundreds of Web addresses; some of these are from cultural partners and offer support alongside the text itself, others are intended for learners abroad and offer insight into how the themes of literature are explored in other places. ALL volunteers have offered some reviews of these links also. The home page now hosts also an occasional feature where a language teacher selects his or her favourite contributions.

# The strategies 3: broadening thinking

The wiki section called 'Pedagogy and research' (http://all-literature.wikidot.com/pedagogy-and-research) is an approximate grouping of documentation from teachers and academics while 'Other reading' includes projects and wider texts.

Among the recent reports and projects, there are some which reflect on the nature of the interactions that teachers have with authentic texts when working with their classes.

The European project 'TALES: Stories for Learning' identifies the importance of the story in the developing minds of children and suggests in its manual (COMENIUS, 2015) (available to read on the website) a variety of ways of using story to convey all sorts of curriculum content and to develop language (http://www.storiesforlearning.eu/?lang=en).

Such projects serve to broaden out language teachers' thinking on their own classroom practice and to build positive connections between practice in primary/secondary classrooms or between practice in supplementary/complementary schools (teaching community heritage or world languages) and mainstream contexts. Some teachers will find certain items controversial but still interesting.

## Window on research

http://tprstories.com/what-is-tprs/ (Rowan, 2017)

This American website (Total Physical Response Stories) features a Krashen-based approach to interaction between teacher and pupils in the context of storytelling with links to IJFLT (International Journal of Foreign Language Teaching). The approach is an extension of the Total Physical Response methodology and is summarized thus:

Blaine Ray found … that changing from commands to the third person singular allowed him to tell stories, a long-term memory technique. He found that asking the students to act out the parts of the characters in the stories preserved the highly effective physical element that had been so powerful in Classical TPR. As the technique was developed over the years, it became an all-encompassing method and methodology. The method combines Dr. James Asher's Total Physical Response (TPR) with Dr. Stephen Krashen's language acquisition strategies, allowing us to teach grammar, reading and writing along with vocabulary.

By simply taking the words being taught, and utilizing gestures, stories, personalized mini situations and personalized questions and answers, TPRS fits seamlessly into a standard language course.

As outlined above, the classroom language teacher's concern will be primarily about the contribution of any text or learning activity to the progress of learners with their knowledge, understanding and use of the language, and the learner's motivation is clearly significant in this progress.

The research of Dörnyei (1994) gives a helpful focus for reflection on this matter. His article 'Motivation and Motivating in the Foreign Language Classroom' (FIFP) includes a section on HOW TO MOTIVATE L2 LEARNERS which is pertinent.

Dörnyei finds that teachers can 'increase the attractiveness of the course content by using authentic materials that are within students' grasp' (281) and through including 'unusual and exotic supplementary materials, recordings, and visual aids' (282). This is relevant to the decision to include in the wiki versions of texts in different media (audio, text, photographic and video, especially resources available online) to make a multisensory impact on our learners' attention – they can follow a written text with the voice recording of a native speaker, or a video performance, or they can follow a spoken text with an animation.

Furthermore, he focusses teachers' attention on an issue which would be very significant to the ALL Literature wiki's development and is reflected in the pro forma above, when he reports on findings that teacher can 'arouse and sustain curiosity and attention by introducing unexpected, novel, unfamiliar, and even paradoxical events; not allowing lessons to settle into too regular a routine; periodically breaking the static character of the classes by changing the interaction pattern'. He recommends 'varied and challenging activities', 'imaginative elements that will engage students' emotions' and 'personalising tasks by encouraging students to engage in meaningful exchanges' – all of which teachers involved in submitting resources to the wiki have taken note of and indeed taken further in their own way.

The findings stimulate teachers to consider establishing a bank of methodological approaches linked to different genres of text, approaches which reflect the nature and mood of the original text. Thus, an amusing text might have a more light-hearted activity than an emotionally charged one; a text which is largely conveying information may work best with a factually based activity, while a narrative text may be suited to a performance type of activity, etc.

As a language teacher, my thoughts are as follows:

'Authentic materials that are within the students' grasp' reflects the notion above that either the text or the activity needs to be age-appropriate; it is quite possible to use a high-level text but devise an 'easier' activity – identifying the gist, spotting key words, reading a passage aloud, providing a title, etc.

'Engag(ing) students' emotions' is a critical motivational contribution that literature could make to learning if carefully handled, as its original purpose is that very engagement.

'Changing the interaction pattern' is the focus for a later section of this chapter; as the contents of the ALL Literature wiki continue to develop, it is interesting to observe the diversity of activities suggested; the digest of some of the principle strategies (along with specific examples) included below may be useful for teachers planning to integrate more authentic/literary texts in their scheme of work.

# The strategies 4: dissemination

Once the ALL Literature wiki was launched, the working group sent regular reminders to ALL members of the growing content via the email newsletter and publications of the association and arranged events to demonstrate the wiki and engage teachers and trainee teachers in contributing; this is an ongoing task, of course. In recognition of the development funding provided, the group also created a version of the wiki entirely in French which is linked to the FIPF international portal so that teachers of French around the world have access and can contribute to the international professional community (http://fipf-litterature.wikidot.com/).

Subsequently ALL as an association was successful in a bid for government funding to provide local training in certain parts of the UK around the issue of the 'new curriculum'; key stage 3 Literature was one of the focus points for this project (called ALL Connect) which leaves a legacy of training modules. The Literature module (available from https://allconnectblog.wordpress.com/category/ks3-literature/) includes substantial examples from, and references to, the Literature wiki. As well as the Module Presentation, there are follow-up activities to help departments develop action plans on the theme of integrating Literature into their schemes.

# The strategies 5: identifying a bank of activities

ALL has a national network of local groups that holds meetings for members according to local need; the working group was able to engage with these groups, and run other events, to encourage discussion on the theme of exploiting text and collate advice to others beginning to consider how to implement the use of literary or authentic texts in their lessons: http://all-literature.wikidot.com/advice.

Language teachers at different levels use texts for exposure to authentic language and for interaction with language in an authentic literary context; they also, in the broader learning context, want their learners to respond to a story, song or poem, for example, with opinions, to understand detail, tone or humorous effect; to take inspiration for new writing; and even to appreciate crafted language.

Some teachers identify a sequenced route into discovery of the text, progressing through strategies which begin with identifying the purpose of the text, spotting of cognates and known language, to the noting of high-frequency structures, which could be recycled by the learners. They may encourage learners to think about the whole text, and more than its vocabulary and grammar, through speculation on tone or meaning (especially if using a mixed media input such as a video clip) before any dictionary work and note-taking; they may also include précis or very short translation activities to identify the gist or key words of a text, and all of these steps may precede personalized productive work.

The text might be a news item from a magazine or website, the lyric of a song, an advert, a poem or a paragraph from a story – and each text type might open the way to approach different outcomes:

- Revisiting or expanding vocabulary
- Observing how description is used
- Noting grammatical features or idiom
- Stimulating expression of opinions or comparisons
- Training one or more of the four skills
- Building confidence, for example, by asking for the gist, or for spot translations of individual words (familiar or cognate or contextualized)

Resources which teachers find especially useful alongside text include visual art to develop cultural or social awareness and connect Language lessons with wider experience and learning; some teachers work with colleagues in a cross-curricular way with texts, for example, on a First World War theme.

Decoding and understanding the written text is often supported by identifying an audio file or a link to a video clip.

Songs, in audio and lyric form, are often popular across the age range, lending themselves to listening, joining in, following the text or training the memory (often unconsciously).

Colleagues also shared practical suggestions for classroom practice such as:

'10 activities for exploiting a text' to be found as a downloadable attached file here: http://all-literature.wikidot.com/pedagogy-and-research

This identifies these key aims of designing text-based activities:

- Build up a bank of knowledge about links between the target language and the mother tongue.

- Talk explicitly about reading strategies – context, breaking words down.
- Use text to teach, not to test.
- Focus for progress checks in plenaries should be the following: 'What new words and phrases have you learnt from the text that you will be able to use in your own work?' List from memory.
- Think-pair-share and group collaboration work well with text activities, particularly if students are encouraged to think about strategies used for code-breaking.
- False friends need to be stored somewhere.
- Activities can usefully focus around discussion about text, not around writing.

# The strategies 6: playing with text

At cross-phase meetings in ALL Local groups, discussion sometimes explores the perception that teachers in primary classrooms are accustomed to planning from the whole text, whereas in secondary classrooms language teachers may be more accustomed to beginning at word level and then progressing through phrase, sentence levels before looking at a full text.

## Reflection

What are the potential advantages in starting from a longer text, rather than individual lexical items?
What are the implications for planning this sort of lesson?

As colleagues develop professional confidence in handling texts constructively, the range of appropriate activities expands to include reading/listening/viewing and the following broad headline strategies:

**Personalizing:** Perhaps the most common strategy used with texts is to ask learners to produce their own version of the original, using their own lives and experiences as the basis: clearly biographical texts are used in this way, as are opinion survey texts, list poems or video presentations.

**Extending:** The basic idea of extending applies especially to writing and requires the learners to continue the text in their own words; it works well with a text in the form of an interview, or a narrative, especially one with built-in repetition.

**Transposing:** The notion here is that the learners convert the original text into a different genre: they read (and/or listen to) a short anecdote and then write (or voice-record) it as a news report; they read a poem and write it as a factual text, or conversely they dramatize a factual text, for example.

Transposing can also be a linguistic task, such as 'desk editing' – rewriting (part of) the text in a different person; for example, if the text is 'I', rewrite it as 'he/she'.

**Adapting:** Students read/view an interview with a famous person and then invent their own interview with another person, recycling some of the questions and structures extracted from the original text but with personal input.

**Interpreting/translating:** This is an area for development in Language classrooms, especially given the extent of the ability range in our schools and the general perception of translation as a fairly technical (i.e. potentially exclusive) activity. To make the habit of translating more inclusive, teachers might focus on short pieces of language within a text: learners identify, for example, the words they think are in the chorus of a song and then work collaboratively to interpret their meaning.

Learners might also be asked how they could change a phrase or sentence to mean something slightly different – the change could be an item of vocabulary or a grammatical element.

**Recycling:** In the context of the new examination requirements, building long-term memory and a personal repertoire of language is a considerable challenge. The value of a literary text is that it includes authentic language of a much wider nature than much language designed for a coursebook. Learners can be encouraged to identify for themselves words they like the look or sound of and begin to use them in their own productive work. Such words can, in early stages, usefully be targeted as – verbs I like, adverbs I like, adjectives I like, etc.

The notion of Recycling may also include development of literacy/oracy skills: the class listens to a short reading (online or in class) following the transcript, with a single focus on the phonics of the language (not the meaning). They identify unfamiliar diacritic marks (umlaut, diaeresis, accent, diphthong), unvoiced letter strings or the differences between vowel sounds in English and the target language.

**Performing:** The concept of performing is particularly relevant to the development of language skills at different ages, as it gives a context for improving spoken work, repetition, linking sound and spelling, encouraging role play and imitation. It might involve speaking

- from words – reading aloud
- from prompts – recounting from images
- from memory – reciting
- based on the whole text – summarizing.

# Exploitation strategies with examples from the ALL Literature wiki

These examples have all been contributed to the ALL Literature wiki.

---

**Strategy 1: Personalizing**

| Activities | Example |
| --- | --- |
| Read/view an interview with person Z Invent and write/record your own interview with person X. | https://www.1jour1actu.com/sport/ just-fontaine-interview-54486/ |

**Strategy 1: Personalizing**

Read a story/narrative text and then invent the actions/mimes for the story. Perform the story with one person reading it and another doing the actions, for a younger audience/on video.

http://all-literature.wikidot.com/dataentry:los-reyes

**Strategy 2: Extending**

| Activities | Example |
| --- | --- |
| Make a voiceover in the target language for a film clip, for example, replace the soundtrack for a recipe. | www.youtube.com/watch?v=t8oArrotPr8 www.youtube.com/watch?v=IE50VzCkVLk&NR=1 |
| Add a scene to a story, or add a conversation for a scene not included in the story. | http://all-literature.wikidot.com/ dataentry:schneewittchen-snow-white |

**Strategy 3: Transposing**

| Activities | Example |
| --- | --- |
| Read the original verse, and write it as a prose anecdote. | For example, La Fontaine: *Le Corbeau et le Renard* http://all-literature.wikidot.com/ dataentry:le-corbeau-et-le-renard |
| Choose a scene from a strip cartoon story and enact the scene, using the dialogue in the speech bubbles, adding anything necessary at the beginning or the end to round it off. | |

**Strategy 4: Adapting**

| Activities | Example |
| --- | --- |
| Read the original text and write a new text of a similar style. | For example, La Fontaine *Le Corbeau et le Renard* above |
| Edit a piece of highly structured original text by changing key linguistic items: the verbs, the category of nouns. | Edit one or more of the monthly/seasonal dictons http://all-literature.wikidot.com/dataentry:le-calendrier For example, *Mai frileux: an langoureux.* *Mai fleuri: an réjoui.* *Mai venteux: an douteux.* *S'il pleut à la Sainte-Madeleine Il pleut pendant six semaines.* |

**Strategy 5: Interpreting/translating**

| Activities | Example |
| --- | --- |

Use a dictionary to produce a version in English of (an appropriate part of) a text you like, ideally trying to respect the flow or style of the original.
This could be of the section of a poem or song lyric you learn by heart.

http://all-literature.wikidot.com/dataentry:oradour

Choose a simple list poem. Translate some or all of the key images.
Extend by using the text as a writing frame.

Casa
*Ventanas azules*
*verdes escaleras,*
*muros amarillos*
*con enredaderos,*
*y en el tajadillo*
*palomas caseras.*
Clemencia Laborda
http://all-literature.wikidot.com/dataentry:casa

### Strategy 6: Recycling

**Activities**

**Example**

Teacher highlights to learners some of the language they might find most useful to know, in order, for example, to tell their own stories.

A purpose written text in the style of a story
http://all-literature.wikidot.com/
      dataentry:le-monstre-qui-volait-les-oeufs

Using a simple repetitively structured story, learners develop their memory of significant structures (verbs, time adverbs, idiom).

http://all-literature.wikidot.com/
      dataentry:le-papa-qui-avait-dix-enfants

### Strategy 7: Performing

Read a text/extract aloud, with appropriate pronunciation, intonation, tone of voice, dynamics, etc.
Recite.

*Tournez, tournez, bons chevaux de bois,*
*Tournez cent tours, tournez mille tours,*
*Tournez souvent et tournez toujours,*
*Tournez, tournez au son des hautbois.*
Verlaine
http://all-literature.wikidot.com/dataentry:chevaux-de-bois

Learn a text/extract by heart and recite; record the text on your phone, etc., for someone to listen to.

*Es ragt ins Meer der Runenstein,*
*Da sitz' ich mit meinen Träumen.*
*Es pfeift der Wind, die Möwen schrein,*
*Die Wellen, die wandern und schäumen.*
*Ich habe geliebt manch schönes ind*
*Und manchen guten Gesellen–*
*Wo sind sie hin? Es pfeift der Wind,*
*Es schäumen und wandern die Wellen.*
Heine
http://all-literature.wikidot.com/
      dataentry:pfeifen-des-windes

---

**Strategy 1: Personalizing**

---

| | |
|---|---|
| Modernize the tongue twister. | http://all-literature.wikidot.com/dataentry:rongrakatikatong |
| The challenge/humour of the text is in its verbal complexity. | |
| Begin from the lyrics, revealing each line slowly and asking the class to read it aloud chorally. | |
| Once a verse is complete, read aloud in pairs – first a full line, then a couplet, then the verse. | |
| Then offer the big challenge of matching the original. | |
| Play a section of the video clip and ask class to follow the words. | |
| Play again and ask class to join in chorally. | |

---

Earlier in the chapter, the point was made that Language lessons are very busy and that the teacher is expected to deliver outcomes in a range of areas (vocabulary, phonetics, grammar, the four skills, culture, literacy, etc.)

It is therefore invaluable to identify texts which can deliver several of these outcomes within a cohesive and concentrated period of time.

There are examples of such 'superactivity' texts also on the Literature wiki:

---

**Superactivity 1**

---

| | |
|---|---|
| **Review, compile, record, explain** As part of an off-timetable activity or end-of-term project, learners make a class anthology. Their tasks are to: Choose a poem from a selection. Type it up accurately. Record a reading. Write a line on why they chose it (in the target language). Write a line on what they think it is about (in the target language). Select a favourite line to translate. | http://all-literature.wikidot.com/dataentry:anthologie-poetique |

---

This activity includes personal choice and performance, speaking, reading and a form of writing, translation and expressing opinion.

| Superactivity 1 | http://all-literature.wikidot.com/ dataentry:un-hombre-sin-cabeza |
|---|---|
| **Playing with text** Teacher displays the first lines of the poem (opposite) and shows enough lines for learners to see the structure. Teacher (or other person) reads the lines aloud. Class reads chorally the lines on screen. Class brainstorms words they know and can guess, building up an interpretation. Class brainstorms one or two ideas for the next lines of the poem (i.e. infinitives of verbs). Learners write the next few lines of the poem themselves, using reference. Class selects the best lines to complete the poem with – display. Teacher reveals the full original poem for discussion. | *Un hombre sin cabeza* *no puede usar sombrero.* *Pero éste no es* *su mayor problema:* *no puede pensar,* *no puede leer* . . . Armando José Sequera |

This text invites Language work with particular focus on extending, interpreting, performance, the four skills and an observation of Grammar.

The ALL Literature wiki continues to grow, and to be discovered by teachers, and new contributions are always welcome. At the time of writing, colleagues around the UK are contributing also to a version of the resource, focused on A level. These repositories will always be work in progress as they are maintained and nourished entirely by volunteer efforts, but that in no way diminishes their value, which we already know from feedback to be considerable.

In conclusion, the process of creating, designing and collating contributions to the wiki continues to be a celebration of professional generosity in the service of the students in our classrooms. As colleagues who attend conferences, local meetings and seminars regularly already know, language teachers are remarkably willing to share their experiences and successes with others; the ALL Literature wiki has benefited from this professional generosity, as teachers pass on advice and recommendations to future generations of people involved in our remarkable task of developing language, cultural curiosity and international experiences for our learners.

Teachers supporting teachers … inspiring language learners.

# References

ALL, the Association for Language Learning (2018). Online at www.ALL-Languages.org.uk, accessed 17 March 2018.

Collins, P. (2012). 'Cross-Curricular Learning in the Secondary School. Worcester Journal of Learning and Teaching', (7): 24–7. Online. https://eprints.worc.ac.uk/1640/1/Phil_Collins_Cross_Curricular_Learning_in_the_Secondary_School.pdf, accessed 17 March 2018.

Comenius (LLP) Lifelong Learning programme (2015). *TALES, Stories for Learning in European Schools, Comenius: European Commission.* Online. http://www.storiesforlearning.eu/?page_id=20, accessed 17 March 2018.

DfE (Department for Education) (2013). *Modern Foreign Languages (MFL): Programme of Study.* London: Department for Education, National Archives. Online. http://webarchive.nationalarchives. gov.uk/20140107102356/http://www.education.gov.uk/schools/teachingandlearning/curriculum/ secondary/b00199616/mfl/programme, accessed 17 March 2018.

DfE (Department for Education) (2014). *National Curriculum, the National Curriculum for England to Be Taught in All Local-Authority-Maintained Schools.* London: Department for Education. Online. https://www.gov.uk/government/collections/national-curriculum, accessed 17 March 2018.

DfE (Department for Education) (2013). *Statutory Guidance: National Curriculum in England: Languages Programmes of Study: Key Stage 2 and Key Stage 3.* London: Department for Education. Online. https://www.gov.uk/government/publications/national-curriculum-in-england-languages- progammes-of-study/national-curriculum-in-england-languages-progammes-of-study, accessed 17 March 2018.

Dobson, A. (2018). 'Towards "MFL for all" in England: A Historical Perspective'. *The Language Learning Journal,* 46(1): 71–85. DOI: 10.1080/09571736.2017.1382058.

Dornyei, Z. (1994). 'Motivation and Motivating in the Foreign Language Classroom'. *The Modern Language Journal,* 78(3) (Autumn, 1994): 273–84.

FIPF (Fédération Internationale des Professeurs de Français). Online. http://fipf.org/, accessed 17 March 2018.

OFSTED (2015). *Research and Analysis: Key Stage 3: The Wasted Years? Ofsted Survey Report Investigating Whether Key Stage 3 Is Providing Pupils with Sufficient Breadth and Challenge.* London: OFSTED. Online. https://www.gov.uk/government/publications/key-stage-3-the-wasted-years, accessed 17 March 2018.

OFSTED (2011). *Research and Analysis: Modern Languages: Achievement and Challenge 2007 to 2010.* London: OFSTED. Online. https://www.gov.uk/government/publications/modern-languages- achievement-and-challenge-2007-to-2010. accessed 17 March 2018.

OFSTED (2008). *The Changing Landscape of Languages: An Evaluation of Language Learning 2004/2007.* London: OFSTED. Online. http://dera.ioe.ac.uk/8192/1/The%20changing%20 landscape%20of%20languages%20%28PDF%20format%29.pdf, accessed 17 March 2018.

QCA (Qualifications and Curriculum Authority) (2004). *Modern Foreign Languages in the Key Stage 4 Curriculum.* London: Qualifications and Curriculum authority. Online. archive.teachfind.com/ qcda/orderline.qcda.gov.uk/gempdf/1847212859.PDF, accessed 17 March 2018.

Rowan, K. (2017). *TPRS – Teaching Proficiency through Reading and Storytelling*. Online. http://tprstories.com/about/, accessed 17 March 2018.

Sell, J. P. A. (2015). 'Why Teach Literature in the Foreign Language Classroom? Universidad de Alcalá, Encuentro 15', *Journal of Research and Innovation in the Language Classroom*, in Section 2. Online. https://ebuah.uah.es/dspace/bitstream/handle/10017/573/11_Sell.pdf?sequence=1, accessed 17 March 2018.

Simons, J. and Porter, N. (2015). *Knowledge and the Curriculum: A Collection of Essays to Accompany E. D. Hirsch's Lecture at Policy Exchange*. London: Policy Exchange. Online. https://policyexchange.org.uk/wp-content/uploads/2016/09/knowledge-and-the-curriculum.pdf, accessed 17 March 2018.

Smith, R. and McLelland, N. (2018). 'Histories of Language Learning and Teaching in Europe'. *The Language Learning Journal*, 46(1): 1–5. DOI: 10.1080/09571736.2017.1382051.

# Index